Differentiated
Science
Inquiry

This book is dedicated to Katie who inquires every day about the world around her.
And to her parents, Janice and Rob, who nurture and support her curiosity.

Differentiated
Science
Inquiry

Douglas
Llewellyn

CORWIN
A SAGE Company

For information:

Corwin
A SAGE Company
2455 Teller Road
Thousand Oaks, California 91320
(800) 233-9936
Fax: (800) 417-2466
www.corwin.com

SAGE Ltd.
1 Oliver's Yard
55 City Road
London EC1Y 1SP
United Kingdom

SAGE India Pvt. Ltd.
B 1/I 1 Mohan Cooperative
  Industrial Area
Mathura Road, New Delhi 110 044
India

SAGE Asia-Pacific Pte. Ltd.
33 Pekin Street #02-01
Far East Square
Singapore 048763

Printed in the United States of America

Library of Congress Cataloging-in-Publication Data

Llewellyn, Douglas.
Differentiated science inquiry / Douglas J. Llewellyn.
    p. cm.
Includes bibliographical references and index.
ISBN 978-1-4129-7503-2 (pbk. : alk. paper)
    1. Science—Study and teaching (Elementary) 2. Science—Study and teaching (Middle school) 3. Elementary school teaching. 4. Middle school teaching. 5. Effective teaching. I. Title.

LB1585.L55 2011
507.1—dc22   2010029356

This book is printed on acid-free paper.

10 11 12 13 14 10 9 8 7 6 5 4 3 2 1

Acquisitions Editor:	Cathy Hernandez
Associate Editor:	Allison Scott
Production Editor:	Cassandra Margaret Seibel
Copy Editor:	Jeannette K. McCoy
Typesetter:	C&M Digitals (P) Ltd.
Proofreader:	Cheryl Rivard
Indexer:	Terri Corry
Cover Designer:	Michael Dubowe
Permissions Editor:	Karen Ehrmann

Contents

Preface

AN ANIMAL SCHOOL

Once upon a time, the grown-up animals of the forest decided they needed to properly educate their youngsters to successfully cope with the ever-increasing demands of living in a woodland community. Faced with the prospect of human invasion, the animal elders met at the local stream. After squabbling among themselves as to what to do, they ultimately decided that they needed to start a school. Days later, a committee was formed to write the learning standards and curriculum for all the animals of the forest. The subjects consisted of running, climbing, swimming, and flying. It was expected that *all* the animals were to meet the competence level for *all* the subjects.

The duck proved to be excellent at swimming, better, in fact, than his teacher. The duck also did pretty well in flying but proved to be well below standards in running. Since he was so poor in running, his teacher made him stay after school to practice running. The duck argued that running didn't fit his needs and interests. Eventually, he even had to drop swimming (his favorite subject) to improve his running skills.

The rabbit started out at the top of her class in running but had anxiety attacks when it came time for swimming lessons. The rabbit always asked for a pass to the nurse's office just before swimming class was about to begin. The rabbit also abhorred climbing and flying classes since she was afraid of heights. She petitioned the school principal to be excused from these subjects, but her request was immediately denied.

The squirrel was excellent in climbing and above average in running but had a fear of flying. He said he had a cousin that was good at flying, but he wasn't. The squirrel also petitioned the principal, asking if leaping could be substituted for flying. The squirrel demonstrated that he could leap from tree limb to tree limb, but his petition too was denied. At the end of the semester, the squirrel received a C in climbing and an F in flying. The squirrel felt he received a lower grade in climbing because by going to the principal he had angered the teacher.

The Animal School story is adapted from an earlier version believed to be written in the 1940s by George H. Reavis, Assistant Superintendent of Schools in Cincinnati, Ohio.

The eagle was the school's star flyer. During climbing class, she would fly to the top of the tree instead of climbing; all the other animals accused her of cheating. The eagle insisted that she could get there any way she chose as long as she got to the top of the tree. Another petition to the principal's office resulted in another denial. On his report card, the eagle got an A in flying but a D in climbing.

The groundhog disliked school because digging was not part of the curriculum. He detested all the approved subjects and eventually stopped attending classes because he was failing everything. The groundhog asked the animal elders if the school could have an extracurricular class in digging. The groundhog even volunteered to teach the class. The elders refused his offer, explaining that digging wasn't part of the curriculum. Knowing that he would have little or no chance to successfully petition his cause to the principal, the groundhog just decided to drop out of school.

Although you may have already heard or read versions of this story before, take a few minutes to think about the significance of the story. If you are with colleagues, share and discuss your responses together. If you are alone, write some comments in the margin that express what you are thinking.

Consider the following questions:

- What does the story tell us about the reality of school for scores of today's elementary, middle, and high school students?
- How does the story depict many of the schools and classrooms we teach in today?
- How does the story reflect the growing needs of individual students, especially those with special learning needs?
- How do high-stakes statewide assessments drive instruction in local school districts?

The purpose of the story is to introduce the need for differentiated teaching based on students' needs and levels of interest and readiness. In most science classes across the country, it is the teacher (not the student) who decides what topic will be taught, what teaching method is appropriate for the topic, and how learners will demonstrate their understandings. Teachers and administrators have control over 99% of the school day—from when and how learning will occur, to when a student can eat lunch, sharpen a pencil, or even go to the bathroom. Unfortunately, students have very little say in school matters. These common traditions are often dictated by district expectations, economic resources, the growing number of students assigned to any particular classroom, or, most assuredly, the attitudes and beliefs of teachers that control what needs to be maintained to ensure a safe and secure classroom environment.

THE PURPOSE OF THIS BOOK

This book proposes that, contrary to this commonly accepted practice of "one-size-fits-all" instruction, teachers can frequently modify their time-honored activities to make them more or less structured, as well as more or less inquiry oriented. Driven by students' range of learning styles, the purpose of this book is to take the reader into the "why's and how's" of differentiating science hands-on activities—especially those categorized as "inquiry-based." The book will also suggest times when it is appropriate for the teacher to choose the instructional strategy and other times when the students can have a choice in the way they learn best. This will be accomplished by introducing a rationale for Differentiated Science Inquiry (DSI) in Part I of the book and providing numerous "pathways to inquiry" with examples of lessons in life, earth, and physical science in Part II.

After reading this book, you will conclusively be able to *identify* when it is most appropriate to differentiate a science inquiry and how to *transform* many of your already favorite conventional activities and labs into a variety of approaches to inquiry.

BALANCING MEANING AND MECHANICS

Science teachers recognize the importance of the concept of balance. Balance is a universal phenomenon in understanding our natural world—whether it's studying a balanced ecosystem, balancing a chemical equation, or considering the notion of opposing forces in stability within the geological world. As humans, we understand the need for a healthy, fit balance within our own bodies as well as keeping our personal checkbook balanced for a means of judging or deciding when we can and can't afford to buy that expensive item.

As complementary forces tend to balance one another, it is the position of this author that exemplary inquiry-based science teachers should be able to articulate not only *how* they do inquiry but also *why* they do it. By balancing *meaning* (the why) and *mechanics* (the how), teachers are in a better position to convey to their colleagues, students, parents, school administrators, and community stakeholders the benefits of teaching and learning through scientific inquiry. In this case, knowing *why* something's important is just as vital as knowing *how* to do what's important. Think of it as the juxtapositional balance of theory and practice: the equilibrium of minds-on coupled with hands-on. Or imagine it as the yin and yang of inquiry.

To help enlighten this notion, after an introduction that briefly revisits the definition of scientific inquiry, this book is divided into two sections. Part I includes the "why" in Chapters 1 through 5, while Part II includes the "how" in Chapters 6 through 10. Chapter 1, "Pathways to Inquiry," classifies various approaches teachers can use to engage their students in inquiry-based learning. The approaches that can lead students into inquiry explorations include demonstrated inquiries and discrepant events, structured inquiries, guided inquiries or problem-solving situations, and self-directed or student-initiated inquiries. The advantages and appropriateness of each approach are described in detail.

Chapter 2, "The Art and Science of Inquiry," builds upon the "Invitation to Inquiry Grid" introduced in *Inquire Within* (Llewellyn, 2007). Although structure and guidance are essential aspects of learning, frequent classroom observations tell us that science teachers too often rely on directed and procedural activities without enabling students to investigate the natural world on their own. In this chapter, an analogy will be drawn paralleling how children learn to paint to how they learn to do science.

Chapter 3 attempts to coin a new term for science educators—"Differentiated Science Inquiry." Chapter 3 dismisses the argument that "one size fits all" and provides a counterargument based on the logic and underlying principles for differentiating science inquiry.

Chapter 4, "Why Teachers Differentiate Science Instruction," introduces the reader to background on students' varied learning styles and how tiered assignments, scaffolding, and flexible groupings help meet students' individual learning needs.

Chapter 5, "Motivation: The Key to Unlock Learning," asks the question: Why are students more engaged in investigating their questions than those given to them by the teacher? The answer lies in "ownership." Developing student voice and ownership for investigative questions is a central attribute of science inquiry. This chapter describes how student ownership and choice develop character and competence. The chapter also highlights current research showing that providing choice enhances intrinsic motivation and ultimately leads to self-directed learning and increased academic achievement.

Part II comprises Chapters 6 through 10, where readers are provided with suggestions how to modify an activity or lab into a DSI approach along with examples of lessons tailored to each of the four inquiry approaches in life, earth, and physical sciences. Last, Chapter 10, "Making a Commitment to Differentiated Science Inquiry," tells the story of one high school science teacher and her journey and transformation to DSI.

WHO THIS BOOK IS WRITTEN FOR

This book is written for elementary, middle, and high school teachers who already have a fundamental background and understanding of scientific inquiry. Whereas my previous books, *Inquire Within* and *Teaching High School Science Through Inquiry,* focus on defining and describing scientific inquiry, this book takes the next step in one's professional inquiry journey by illustrating a deeper awareness of the various approaches to science inquiry and how teachers in Grades 3 through 12 can adapt and facilitate an array of inquiry methodologies geared toward meeting the diverse instructional needs of their students.

This book has multiple audiences. It is written for teachers studying about scientific inquiry in either an advanced undergraduate or graduate-level methods course. The book is likewise geared to those participating in a summer science institute or teacher-leaders and experienced science specialists that coach and mentor novice and apprentice-level teachers through their own inquiry journeys. Others might use *Differentiated Science Inquiry* as a book study within a collegial support group or a literature circle as a way to extend their work in scientific inquiry. Reading and reflecting on the chapters, examples, and vignettes is an excellent way to develop a professional learning community of inquirers.

Last, but equally important, are those science teachers pursuing National Board Certification for Early Adolescence (ages 11–15). Developing and implementing a lesson centered on differentiated science inquiry provides a novel means to demonstrate competence for your portfolio submission for the standard "Advancing Student Learning—Science Inquiry."

Regardless of how it's used, this book is for the science educator who considers him- or herself (as I do) a "student of inquiry" and desires to advance one's proficiency for inquiry-based teaching to a new level. Toward that purpose, I hope you will find the "voice" of this book to be sounding more like a coach or a mentor than of an expert trying to impart knowledge to the reader. Now, if you're ready, let's get started.

Acknowledgments

I gratefully appreciate the contribution and support from many gifted colleagues and friends in writing this book. Some were a source of inspiration, some provided a "voice" that helped shape my understanding of differentiation and inquiry, and some provided editing and writing assistance. Thanks to all of you.

A tip of the cap goes out to the following:

- Ron Bailey for editing the Animal School story
- Edwina Farnand for sharing the painting analogy
- Kathryn Franz and her fourth-grade class for field-testing the Grades 3–6 Preference Survey
- Beth Jackelen and her class at French Road Elementary School for field-testing the Balls and Ramps activity
- Shelby Koheler for field-testing the Grades 7–12 Preference Survey with her science classes at Berger Middle School
- Jeff Marshall for commenting on early chapters and providing advice and encouragement
- Lisa Moosbrugger and Steve Orcutt for inviting me to present at their summer science workshop and field-test the Balls and Ramps activity
- JoAnn Morreale for sharing the Stream Tables activity
- Leonard Ortenzi for trying to teach a former biology major the physics background in the Balls and Ramps activity
- Bernard Ricca for providing content background on the Balls and Ramps activity
- Rob Sanford for inviting me to visit and observe his fifth-grade classroom
- Debbie Stack for editing every chapter and verse of the manuscript before submission
- John Travers for editing early drafts and offering collegial cheer
- Cathy Hernandez at Corwin for providing continued assistance and encouragement

In addition, Corwin gratefully acknowledges the contributions of the following reviewers:

Regina Brinker
Science Teacher
Christensen Middle School
Livermore, CA

About the Author

 Like many of you, **Douglas Llewellyn** wears several hats. One hat is his teaching hat. Doug teaches science education and educational leadership courses at St. John Fisher College (Rochester, NY). Previously, he was the K–12 Director of Science at the Rochester City School District, a junior high school principal, and a middle school science teacher. Recently he codirected a program to develop K–12 teacher-leaders in mathematics and science. Llewellyn's research interests are in the areas of scientific inquiry, constructivist teaching, and teacher leadership.

His second hat is his author and presenter hat. He writes on science education and leadership for the National Science Teachers Association and other professional journals. Llewellyn is a frequent speaker at state and national science conferences on constructivist and inquiry-based teaching. His book, *Inquire Within: Implementing Inquiry-Based Science Standards in Grades 3–8*, Second Edition, is published by Corwin. Accompanying his *Inquire Within* book is a *Facilitator's Guide* to help science leaders and coordinators plan effective professional development in science inquiry. His Grades 9–12 book, *Teaching High School Science Through Inquiry*, is copublished by Corwin and NSTA.

His third and favorite hat is his Boston Red Sox cap. During the summer months, he is usually either watching a baseball game or boating on the New York State Finger Lakes and the Erie Canal. He can be reached at dllewellyn@sjfc.edu or dllewell@rochester.rr.com.

Introduction

THREE MODELS OF INSTRUCTION

There are numerous instructional models that educators refer to. However, to develop a grasp of differentiated science inquiry, we will build a context for inquiry by first identifying and explaining three prevailing models of instruction familiar to most teachers of science: the Direct Instruction model, the Mastery Learning model, and the 5E Learning Cycle. Before we go any further, it should be noted that one model is not more desirable than another. Each has its own purpose and place in the classroom. It is the teacher who should be cognizant of each model and choose the best model for the situation. With that said, let's move on.

On one end of the spectrum, the *Direct Instruction* model is a conventional, scripted approach commonly used in science, especially in teaching process skill acquisition and development (observing, classifying, inferring, predicting, and identifying and controlling variables). Direct Instruction (DI) was first introduced to educators by Sigfried Englemann in the 1960s and became popularized in teaching basic mathematical calculations and computations. Drill and practice in mathematics is a common procedure still used today by teachers, especially those in elementary schools.

DI involves a structured, practice-based, behaviorist methodology where the teacher introduces the topic and then provides directed teaching, usually in the form of a brief oral presentation or a visual demonstration, followed by a period where students practice the skill under the guidance and supervision of the teacher. During the guided practice phase, the teacher assesses the students' work and assists in making corrections and providing additional instruction as needed. Following the guided practice, students then move on to work independently to further reinforce the content or skills being taught. In some cases, the independent practice may take the form of homework. Additional time for closure and review concludes the DI model.

On the opposite end of the spectrum is the *Learning Cycle*. The Learning Cycle was first conceived as "guided discovery" by Myron Atkins and Robert Karplus in 1962. The model was later refined and reintroduced by Robert Karplus and Herbert Thier (1967) in the late 1960s. The Karplus-Thier model centered on three phases of teaching science: Exploration, Concept Attainment, and Application. It later became the instructional foundation for a revolutionary, new science program—SCIS, the Science Curriculum Improvement Study. During the Exploration phase, students experienced a particular science phenomenon, usually as a hands-on activity. That was followed by the introduction of terms and vocabulary associated with the phenomenon being explored. The Application phase then allowed students to apply their new knowledge to new situations. The Learning Cycle, which models a constructivist approach, was redesigned in the 1980s into the 5E Learning Cycle by the Biological Science Curriculum Study (BSCS) of Colorado Springs, Colorado. The 5E model comprises five stages or phases: Engagement, Exploration, Explanation, Extension (or Elaboration), and Evaluation. The 5E Learning Cycle was adapted for the earlier version with two new phases added on the beginning (Engagement) and the end (Evaluation). The 5E model is most closely associated with inquiry-based teaching and learning. It is particularly useful in developing skills, content, and conceptual understandings.

During the Engagement stage, the teacher initiates the learning task and sets the objective of the lesson, assesses students' prior knowledge, and focuses students' attention on the learning outcomes of the lesson. This is usually accomplished by demonstrating the main concept to be learned through attention-getting modes and discrepant events, and providing a "cognitive hook" as a motivation for learning.

After capturing students' attention, the teacher provides an opportunity for the class to explore and investigate a phenomenon providing a common base of experience during the Exploration stage. The exploration involves students observing, wondering, and posing questions.

During the Explanation stage, the teacher has the students communicate their observations and explanations from the Engagement and the Exploration stages. The teacher then introduces, explains, and reinforces concepts, processes, and appropriate vocabulary terms. Throughout this stage, students make meaning of their previous experiences and attach significance and relevance. Most importantly, vocabulary and terms are presented *after* students have an opportunity to explore and discover, as opposed to preteaching vocabulary, out of context, *before* the exploration. The Explanation stage is also an appropriate time for the teacher to address students' misconceptions that were uncovered during the Engagement and Exploration stages.

The Extension or Elaboration stage extends and applies the students' conceptual understanding to situations beyond the classroom. This stage assists in making real-world applications to the topic as well as applying knowledge to new situations and inquiries. During the Extension stage, students develop a deeper elaboration and understanding of concepts and are encouraged to investigate additional questions raised during the earlier stages of the model.

In the final stage, Evaluation, the teacher assesses students' understandings through traditional and alternative assessment strategies and/or performance tasks and determines the progress made toward achieving the learning objectives. Although the Evaluation stage implies a degree of formal, summative assessment, in actuality, assessment is an ongoing, formative process throughout the entire cycle. If you are interested in more information and research findings on the 5E instructional model, see "The BSCS 5E Instructional Model: Origins, Effectiveness, and Applications" at http://www.bscs.org/pdf/5EFull%20Report.pdf. A shorter, executive summary is also available on the BSCS website under "BSCS Reports."

Somewhere between the DI model and the 5E Learning Cycle lies the *Mastery Learning* model popularized by Madeline Hunter. The Mastery Learning model provides a blended teaching approach, useful for both skill and content development, and is an input-output-based model that focuses on six distinct steps:

- Stating Learning Objectives
- Anticipatory Set
- Input or Modeling
- Guided Practice
- Checking for Understanding (reteaching if necessary)
- Independent Practice

Similar to the two previously mentioned models, the Mastery Learning model begins with stating the objectives to be learned to inform the purpose for learning, followed by focusing students' attention on the day's learning activity during the Anticipatory Set phase. The Mastery Learning model is similar to the DI model in that they both provide teacher-centered instruction followed by guided and independent levels of practice. The Mastery Learning model, however, includes a phase where the teacher uses various formative assessments to "check for understanding" and provides reteaching when an individual student fails to attain a predetermined level of content mastery, usually at 80%.

The purpose of this section is to emphasize that each instructional model has its distinct advantages. At times, it may be more appropriate to use one model over another. For example, according to the National Science Education Standards (NRC, 2007), "There are times when explicit or direct instruction is a more appropriate choice and will complement inquiry-based teaching, especially when students have already had a great deal of direct experience with a particular phenomenon" (p. 115). By having many instructional strategies available in their toolkit, teachers are most certainly in a better position to differentiate their instruction to fit the needs of their students.

For the purposes of this book, we will emphasize inquiry-based teaching and learning and how it can be best served through models of instruction similar to the 5E Learning Cycle. Using the 5E model, science teachers frequently provide a highly motivating, open-ended inquiry during the Exploration stage and a more focused inquiry for follow-up questions and investigations during the Extension stage. Or to picture it another way, think of providing a structured inquiry during the Exploration stage and a follow-up structured inquiry, a guided inquiry, or a self-directed inquiry during the Extension stage.

As we later discuss differentiated science inquiry and the value of providing choice to students, we will see how inquiry and the 5E model go hand in hand to deliver an exploratory-based science unit of study.

REVISITING THE MEANING
OF SCIENTIFIC INQUIRY

Inquiry is polymorphous. You can easily find many definitions and interpretations of the term. More specifically, science inquiry can exist solely as a minds-on investigation utilizing the Internet, research literature, and other resources. Or it can exist as a combination minds-on and hands-on activity. In the literature, as well as in professional conversations, teachers refer to hands-on or manipulative inquiry in three forms: structured, guided, and full or open inquiry. This author frequently uses the terms *teacher-initiated inquiry* and *student-initiated inquiry* to describe the source of the questions being investigated. Inquiry investigations can be designed as a stand-alone activity, either short term (lasting one or more classroom periods) or long term (lasting a semester or a full academic year). Generally, biological and ecological-based inquiries require longer time to study, whereas many physical science inquiries can be either short term or long term. Besides stand-alone examples, inquiry investigations, as mentioned earlier, can also be integrated into the 5E Learning Cycle, in either the Exploration or the Elaboration stage.

According to the *National Science Education Standards* (NRC, 1996, 2007), science as inquiry has a threefold meaning. It refers not only to students *doing* the act of investigating a scientific phenomenon by making careful observations, analyzing and interpreting data and evidence to support or refute a claim, proposing explanations, and communicating results but also to students *knowing about* the process of scientific inquiries by articulating the nature of science and the reasoning skills involved in their own investigations. Inquiry also refers to teachers *using* inquiry as an instructional approach to teach students both science content and the methods and processes real scientists employ in research labs. For more information on the differences between these three meanings of scientific inquiry, read *Inquiry and the National Science Education Standards* by the National Research Council (2007).

However, in reality, classroom inquiry, the science inquiry that students do in schools, is somewhat different from research inquiry (the inquiry that practicing scientists do in research labs). Time, material resources, lab restrictions, and even high-stakes state assessments are day-to-day challenges facing classroom teachers, often restricting the depth and frequency of teaching science through inquiry.

As you read this book, you may already have a substantial understanding of inquiry. Furthermore, some readers may be more savvy and experienced with the concept of scientific inquiry. Consequently, not everyone needs to read this next section. So, if you think you are reading material that's not new to you, move on to Chapter 1. If you are new to inquiry or want to refresh your memory of scientific inquiry, let's highlight the distinctions among three terms often found in science teaching circles: inquiry, science inquiry, and scientific inquiry.

In the general sense, *inquiry* refers to seeking information, usually through questioning. Inquiry is not new nor is it a fad. It can be traced back to the ancient Greek philosophers as a means of teaching. Socrates (469 BC–399 BC) is often credited as one of the earliest teachers using inquiry through what's commonly called the Socratic Method. Like the Socratic Method, inquiry involves acts of posing and clarifying questions, seeking and collecting evidence, confirming or rejecting suspicions, and communicating the outcome of the question. For the purpose of this book, inquiry will be used as a broad, information-seeking skill that permeates all subject areas. Science does not hold the monopoly on inquiry.

Science inquiry, again for the purpose of this book, will be defined as those activities, explorations, and investigations where students seek answers to questions or problems, posed by either the teacher, the textbook, or the students themselves. Science inquiries are usually classified as structured inquiries, guided inquiries, or student-directed inquiries. Each will be explained in greater detail in Chapter 1. Portions in this book will refer to classroom examples of science inquiry, especially in Chapters 7 through 9.

Finally, *scientific inquiry* involves the knowledge, skills, and attitudes students develop while investigating their natural world. During scientific investigations, these three aspects are integrated and wound together like three strands of a rope. Scientific inquiry also refers to the critical thinking skills that students engage in while undertaking science explorations. According to the National Research Council (NRC) in the *National Science Education Standards,* when describing scientific inquiry, the NRC says, "Inquiry is a multifaceted activity that involves making observations; posing questions; examining books and other sources of information to see what is already known in light of experimental evidence; using tools to gather, analyze, and interpret data; proposing answers, explanations, and predictions; and communicating the results. Inquiry requires identification of assumptions, use of critical and logical thinking, and consideration of alternative explanations" (NRC, 1996, p. 23).

Aligned to the NRC's definition, I have attempted to identify seven segments of scientific inquiry and further subdivide each segment into more specific subtasks (see Figure I.1). Although the segments and subtasks appear as a listed form, the subtasks within each segment are multidirectional. The diverse approaches to inquiry may involve all or some of the tasks, depicting many possible avenues for exploration. The list of tasks should not be construed as a recipe-like process. Whereas the scientific method is usually described by textbooks in terms of separate, sequential steps, not all science inquiries follow a specific route. Teachers of science need to dispel the naive conception that there is one method used by practicing scientists. In science, whether in the research lab or the classroom, different questions require different avenues for investigation.

For example, as we become more sophisticated with the notion of science as inquiry, we realize that some science inquiries may involve writing a hypothesis. Others may not. One inquiry can engage students with making a prediction as to the expected outcome, while another engages students in exploration and discovery leading to form a concluding claim toward the end of the investigation. Some investigations take the form of experiments that involve treatment and control conditions. Again, others may not.

When looking at all the parts of a science inquiry, many teachers seem to emphasize the planning and conducting (see list that follows) segments of experiments as the foremost components of a science inquiry. Similarly, formulating and clarifying an initiating question is an area that students want to gloss over. They naturally want to get to the actual "doing" part of the activity. While planning and conducting aspects of an experiment or an investigation are certainly critical aspects of inquiry, this author contends that on the front end—formulating and clarifying a focused question to investigate—and on the back end—making claims based on the evidence and explaining those claims to others—are elements of scientific inquiry often downplayed due to limited classroom time. Let's now look into the various segments of science inquiry and see how each segment adds to a student's holistic understanding and appreciation for *doing* and learning *about* scientific inquiry.

SEVEN SEGMENTS OF SCIENTIFIC INQUIRY

When students engage in a science inquiry, the investigation can be divided into three major areas: the question, the procedure, and the results. These three areas can be further divided into segments. Each segment has its own distinct set of thinking skills and performance skills, and when viewed collectively, contributes to the spirit of curiosity and discovery. The seven segments of inquiry-based learning include the following:

The Question

    1. Exploring a Phenomenon

    2. Focusing on a Question

The Procedure

    3. Planning the Investigation

    4. Conducting the Investigation

The Results

    5. Analyzing the Data and Evidence

    6. Constructing New Knowledge

    7. Communicating New Knowledge

THE QUESTION

1. Exploring a Phenomenon

- Observe a phenomenon or discrepant event (or engage in an open-ended exploration).
- Assess your prior knowledge about the phenomenon by asking, "What do I know about what's happening?"
- Assess others' prior knowledge about the phenomenon by asking, "What do others know about what's happening?"

2. Focusing on a Question

- Make a list of several questions to investigate from the observations made.
- Choose one (or the first) question to investigate.
- Scrutinize the question by asking, "Is the question investigatable?"
- Modify the question, if necessary.
- Seek initial evidence through additional observations of the phenomenon.
- Clarify the question by asking, "Before designing an investigation, do I completely understand the question?"
- Rewrite the question, if necessary.

THE PROCEDURE

3. Planning the Investigation

- Decide what data need to be collected to answer the question.
- Identify the variables and constants needed to investigate the question.
- Design a controlled experiment or investigation to answer the question.
- Identify the materials needed to carry out the investigation.
- Draw an illustration of the materials and setup for the investigation.
- Propose a hypothesis as to an expected and/or predicted outcome of the investigation.
- Design a chart or table to organize the data to be collected during the investigation.
- Identify safety rules to follow during the investigation.

4. Conducting the Investigation

- Carry out the investigation.
- Collect appropriate data.
- Record data in the proper column of the chart or table.
- Graph the results, if applicable.
- Redesign and retry the investigation, if necessary.

THE RESULTS

5. Analyzing the Data and Evidence

- Interpret and make meaning from the data.
- Determine if the data are biased or flawed in any way.
- Seek patterns and relationships among the variables.
- Draw conclusions based on the data and evidence.
- Analyze the data and evidence to support, modify, or refute the previously stated hypothesis.
- Make a claim based on the evidence collected.

6. Constructing New Knowledge

- Form an explanation (or model) from the claim and supporting evidence.
- Relate the explanation (or model) to other existing models.
- Reflect upon and make meaning as to your newly acquired knowledge.
- Connect new knowledge to your prior knowledge and the knowledge of others.

7. Communicating New Knowledge

- Choose a means to communicate your explanation (or model) and findings to others (i.e., oral report, poster, PowerPoint, written report).
- Discuss your results and conclusions with others.
- Use scientific reasoning skills to link your claim and supporting evidence.
- Engage in scientific argumentation, allowing others to critique your investigation and findings and provide counterclaims to your results.
- Make modifications to your explanation or model, if needed.
- Consider follow-up questions or other questions from Step 4 to investigate.

Figure I.1   Seven Segments of Scientific Inquiry

For some, the list may seem too long—while others may suggest that there are specific cognitive or manipulative performances that need to be explicitly taught and reinforced in order for students to truly become authentic scientific inquirers. In either case, I need to add a disclaimer: Not all inquiries include all the skills and performances listed in the segments.

In addition, do not interpret the skills and performances as sequential "steps" to a science inquiry. As mentioned previously, different questions require different means of investigation. That's a fundamental feature of differentiated science inquiry. At times, the teacher will provide the question, or even the question and the procedure; while other times, the student is responsible for formulating the question, designing a procedure, and concluding the results. Later in the book, we will see how science inquiries can be easily adapted and modified to meet the needs and abilities of your students. These seven segments will be highlighted throughout the book as we enhance our awareness and appreciation into differentiating science instruction.

INQUIRY AS A HUMAN ENDEAVOR

Although the seven segments offer a "progression" for collecting data and forming explanations, the observations made, the claims stated, and evidence collected through student inquiries are seldom identical. Spurred by their inquisitiveness, students' explanations are largely based on their *a priori* experiences and expectations of the event being explored. Sometimes, two students can conduct the same science inquiry yet draw different inferences, claims, and explanations from the same set of observations. In this sense, both sorting evidence and constructing explanations become very personal. As stated in the *Benchmarks for Science Literacy*, the American Association for the Advancement of Science says, "What people expect to observe often affects what they actually do observe" (AAAS, 1993, p. 12).

Furthermore, the National Research Council (2007) states, "Science is very much a human endeavor, and the work of science relies on basic human qualities, such as reasoning, insight, energy, skill, and creativity—as well as on scientific habits of mind, such as intellectual honesty, tolerance of ambiguity, skepticism, and openness to new ideas" (p. 170). As teachers guide their classes through inquiries, it is crucial to remind students to keep accurate records of their work in the interest of objectivity. Younger children may experience varying difficulties being entirely objective about their work. They tend to choose information as evidence to support their point of view. To help thwart sources of bias, the accurate collection of data and information is invaluable in supporting claims that are backed with evidence, logical arguments, and critical reasoning (AAAS, 1993). Throughout the inquiry process, students should be encouraged to exhibit skepticism and act as a "reflective friend" in critiquing each other's conjectures and suppositions. Only through the analysis and examination of each other's work can students truly appreciate the work of scientists and the essence of inquiry.

Part I

The Meaning of Inquiry—The "Why" Chapters

In the Animal School story, we are acquainted with several woodland creatures, each having their own set of survival skills and abilities. Similarly, school-age youngsters and adolescents have their own unique skill set to survive the school's daily schedule. Meeting the diversity of student needs by adapting curricular materials has become a prime emphasis, as well as a challenge, for today's educators. In Part I, we will see why differentiating instruction is now more important than ever before.

Pathways to Inquiry

INVITATION TO INQUIRY

In *Inquire Within* (Llewellyn, 2007), I familiarized readers with several means of inviting students to inquiry-based learning through the Invitation to Inquiry Grid (see Figure 1.1). The invitations are like pathways teachers regularly use to initiate student inquiries. They include (a) demonstrated inquiries and discrepant events, (b) structured inquiries, (c) guided inquiries (also called teacher-initiated inquiries or problem-solving activities), and (d) self-directed inquiries (also called student-initiated or full inquiries). For each approach, the source of the question, the procedure, and the results differ, originating from either the teacher or the student. Whereas demonstrated inquiries and discrepant events are more teacher led, the source of the question and the procedure stems from the teacher. Self-directed and student-initiated inquiries, however, are more student led. Here, the source of the question and the procedure originates from the student. Thus, as one moves from left to right on the grid, the ownership of the question and the procedure shifts from the teacher to the student.

	Demonstrated Inquiry or Discrepant Event	Structured Inquiry	Guided Inquiry or Teacher-Initiated Inquiry	Self-Directed Inquiry or Student-Initiated Inquiry
Posing the question	Teacher	Teacher	Teacher	Student
Planning the procedure	Teacher	Teacher	Student	Student
Analyzing the results	Teacher	Student	Student	Student

Figure 1.1 Invitation to Inquiry

Source: Llewellyn, D. (2007). *Inquire Within: Implementing Inquiry-Based Science Standards in Grades 3–8*, 2nd ed. Thousand Oaks, CA: Corwin.

As we move from left to right on the grid, we also notice how the level of ownership varies. The left side of the grid appears to be more structured and more teacher centered, whereas the right side is less structured and more student centered. Figure 1.2 illustrates the level and significance of ownership. And as any teachers will assert, when students own their question, they engender a feeling of empowerment. We'll address the notion of structure and ownership later in Chapters 4 and 5.

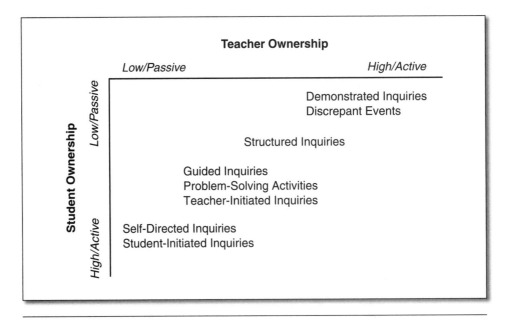

Figure 1.2 Student-Teacher Ownership

As teachers chart their yearlong instructional plans, they take into account the prior experience their students have in scientific inquiry, noting some students may come to class with little or no prior experience, while others possess a wealth of previous experiences in posing their own questions, formulating their own procedures, and collecting and organizing their own results. Experienced inquiry teachers take this into consideration when planning just how and when to introduce inquiry-based opportunities into their courses. For some classes, it may necessitate a gradual transition from left to right on the grid—spending several months on demonstrated inquiry and having students perform structured or guided inquiry activities before moving on to more open-ended investigations. This, of course, is a very natural scaffolding process in learning science through inquiry. For other students more experienced and savvy in self-guided explorations, the shift from left to right occurs more quickly. Thus, each class marks its own progress toward inquiry-based learning.

CATEGORIES OF SCIENCE INQUIRY

Throughout the literature and in professional conversations among elementary, middle, and high school teachers, the terms *discrepant events, structured inquiries, guided inquiries,* and *self-directed* (or open or full) *inquiries* are frequently used. To avoid any confusion, let's describe each of these categories of inquiry.

A *demonstrated inquiry* or discrepant event is a teacher-led presentation focusing on a particular topic or phenomenon geared toward capturing students' attention. What makes them different from traditional demonstrations is that a discrepant event often culminates in an attention-grabbing observation that is counterintuitive to the students' normal understandings. These types of presentation are often thought of as mind-engaging introductions to a new topic that peak interests and challenge prior conceptions. The unexpected results are usually contradictory to students' normal experiences and serve to promote curiosity and motivation for the concept about to be studied. Demonstrated inquiries also serve as a springboard into further questions and follow-up inquiries.

In *structured inquiry,* students engage in a hands-on activity or lab, collect and organize data, and draw conclusions but follow a precise set or sequence of instructions and procedures provided by the teacher or the textbook. In *The Lingo of Learning,* Colburn (2003) describes a structured inquiry as a situation where "the teacher gives students a hands-on problem they are to investigate, and the methods and materials to use for the investigation, but not expected outcomes. Students are to discover a relationship and generalize from the data collected" (p. 20). Despite the negative connotation, structured activities are often mislabeled as cookbook labs, confirmation labs, or verification labs. The distinction between structured inquiries and cookbook labs is that with structured inquiries, the student assumes more responsibility for determining how to collect and organize his or her data, whereas cookbook labs usually provide the student with directions regarding what data to collect and how to collect the data, along with a predetermined chart or table that shows how to fill in the data. I contend that if a student cannot design a data table for an inquiry, he or she probably doesn't completely understand the investigation or the variables being tested. Therefore, one of the foremost ways to modify a traditional cookbook lab into a structured inquiry is to remove the data table and encourage the students to design their own. This simple step will give students more opportunities to analyze and comprehend their results.

A second distinction is that with structured labs, although the procedure is provided, students are responsible for discovering the evidence to support the stated hypothesis (if there is one) and looking for patterns and relationships within the data. Cookbook labs usually suggest the patterns through prompts and fill-in-the-blank-type questions. They are best for compliant learners who depend upon the teacher for direction and affirmation. Colburn (2003) further suggests that in structured inquiries, ". . . students are largely responsible for figuring out what the data might mean—that is, they analyze and interpret the data. . . . In a verification lab, on the other hand, all students are expected to arrive at the same conclusion—there's a definite right answer that students are supposed to be finding during the lab activity" (p. 20). Keep in mind that analyzing evidence and formulating an explanation are essential reasoning skills strengthened through science inquiries.

Whether we call an activity a structured inquiry or a cookbook lab, teachers know that at times and within given situations, students need structure and direction in carrying out their investigations. The key for teachers is to introduce structured investigations but gradually wean students toward more independence. More about the need for structure will come in upcoming chapters.

In *guided inquiry*, the teacher poses the question or the problem to be investigated and suggests the materials to be used while the students, on their own, design and carry out a procedure for the investigation. The students then form conclusions and explanations from the data collected. In this book, guided inquiry is synonymous with problem solving or teacher-initiated inquiry, since the source of the question or problem originates from the teacher.

And last, *self-directed inquiry* is a situation where students generate their own questions concerning a topic or phenomenon and then design their investigations, identify variables, and select and carry out procedures to answer these questions. At the conclusion of the self-directed inquiry, students then propose claims and explanations supported by the evidence collected and communicate the findings to others. Self-directed inquiry accentuates creativity over conformity and helps students create structure from ambiguity.

Since it's sometimes unrealistic to expect students to generate self-directed questions without any frame of reference, these inquiries usually originate from open-ended explorations, demonstrated inquiries, and discrepant events that cause students to wonder and ask, "What would happen if . . . ?" For our discussion, self-directed inquiry is synonymous with student-initiated inquiry, full inquiry, or open inquiry.

In concluding the differences among the categories, let's return to the seven segments of scientific inquiry introduced in the Introduction. For structured inquiries, the question and the procedure portions are orchestrated by the teacher. The students will follow the prescribed directions in the procedure, collect appropriate data, and conclude the results of the investigation. For guided inquiries, the teacher provides the question to be investigated, and the students are responsible for designing and conducting the investigation as well as collecting and analyzing the data and communicating their findings to others. Last, in full inquiries, the students are responsible for all aspects of the investigation: formulating the question, planning and carrying out the procedure, and analyzing and communicating the results. Knowing this, teachers can now take any activity or lab and use the segment list to determine which category the investigation falls under.

WHAT TEACHERS AND STUDENTS DO AT EACH APPROACH TO INQUIRY

We can further our understanding of the different pathways to inquiry by identifying the behaviors demonstrated by teachers and students for each approach. Since each approach in the Inquiry Grid has its own distinctive set of performances, Figures 1.3 through 1.6 help us to distinguish one approach from another. As you read through the descriptions, notice how the responsibility subtly shifts from teacher-led demonstrated inquiries to student-led full inquiries.

Level of Inquiry	What the Teacher Does	What the Student Does
Demonstrated Inquiries and Discrepant Events	• Introduces a new concept by creating awareness and interest • Poses questions and elicits responses to assess students' understanding of the concept • Acts as a motivator by providing observable discrepancies to generate curiosity and inquisitiveness • Generates a "cognitive hook" to a new or abstract concept • Asks students to describe or explain their observations • Models appropriate scientific and safety procedures and processes • Uses "show and tell" modes of instruction	• Connects new observations to prior experiences and knowledge • Takes notes and provides a justifiable explanation to observable phenomenon • Builds and elaborates upon the observations and explanations of others • Shows curiosity and interest by asking "what if" and "how come" questions in response to the demonstration or discrepancy

Figure 1.3 What Teacher or Student Does—Demonstrated

Level of Inquiry	What the Teacher Does	What the Student Does
Structured Inquiries	• Provides step-by-step, sequential procedures to follow • Provides materials and supplies as listed on the activity sheet or lab • Assigns roles to students on a rotating basis • Acts as a coach by ensuring all students are on task and understand the procedure • Encourages students to work as a group • Asks probing questions and answers questions when appropriate • Provides follow-up and "going further" questions and inquiries	• Obtains materials and supplies as listed on the activity sheet or lab • Reads and follows directions according to activity sheet or lab • Uses science process skills to collect data • Communicates and collaborates with other group members • Makes observations, collects data, and records observations • Designs data charts and tables for organizing collected data • Looks for patterns and relationships within the data • Draws conclusions and formulates explanations • Evaluates and communicates the results • Asks new and related questions based on the data collected

Figure 1.4 What Teacher or Student Does—Structured

Level of Inquiry	What the Teacher Does	What the Student Does
Guided Inquiries, Problem-Solving Activities, and Teacher-Initiated Inquiries	• Provides a problem to solve or a question to investigate • Encourages students to design a means to solve the problem or answer the question posed • Acts as a facilitator to the problem-solving process • Makes suggestions for needed equipment and supplies • Encourages accountability and shared decision making among the group members • Poses questions and prompts to extend students' thinking • Directs students to other resources of information related to the problem • Organizes a means for students to communicate their findings and explanations • Assesses students' ability to solve problems	• Defines the nature and the parameters of the problem • Brainstorms and generates possible procedures and solutions to solve the problem • Selects and designs a strategy or plan • Creates models or illustrations of the design • Selects appropriate supplies and equipment needed • Implements the plan to solve the problem • Uses science process skills to collect and analyze information about the problem • Communicates and collaborates with other group members • Makes observations, collects data, and records observations • Designs data charts and tables for organizing collected data • Looks for patterns and relationships within the data • Draws conclusions and formulates explanations • Evaluates and communicates the results • Asks new and related questions based on the data collected

Figure 1.5 What Teacher or Student Does—Guided

Level of Inquiry	What the Teacher Does	What the Student Does
Self-Directed Inquiries and Student-Initiated Inquiries	• Provides an open-ended exploration to initiate questions • Acts as a mentor to assist students to uncover answers and solutions to their questions and problems • Assists in providing needed equipment and supplies	• Makes initial observations and speculations that drive personal questions • Acts as an investigator by stating a question • Takes ownership of the question • Brainstorms and identifies variables related to the question

Level of Inquiry	What the Teacher Does	What the Student Does
	• Poses additional questions and prompts to apply and elaborate students' initial questions • Directs students to other resources of information related to the question or problem • Organizes a means for students to communicate their findings and explanations • Assesses students' ability as self-directed learners	• Constructs a claim, hypothesis, or prediction to test • Designs procedures to answer the question • Determines equipment and supplies needed • Carries out the procedure to acquire data and evidence • Designs data charts and tables for organizing collected data • Organizes the data in the form of a chart or table • Looks for patterns and relationships within the data • Describes the relationship among variables • Determines the validity of the data and evidence • Supports or refuses the claim based on the evidence collected • Draws conclusions and formulates explanations • Evaluates and communicates the results • Asks new and related questions based on the data collected

Figure 1.6   What Teacher or Student Does—Self-Directed

TEACHER POSITIONS AT EACH APPROACH TO INQUIRY

Associated with the observable behaviors of the teacher, we can also describe the physical position the teacher assumes in relation to the students in the room for each approach to inquiry. Figure 1.7 shows the stance the teacher takes for each approach.

During a demonstrated inquiry, the teacher plays the role as a *motivator* and usually assumes a "front-and-center" location so he or she can be easily seen by all the students in the class. Although the teacher may certainly move about during the presentation, the students' attention is centered on the teacher and focused on the demonstration table, usually located at the front of the classroom. In this approach, students are most often seated in typical rows and columns.

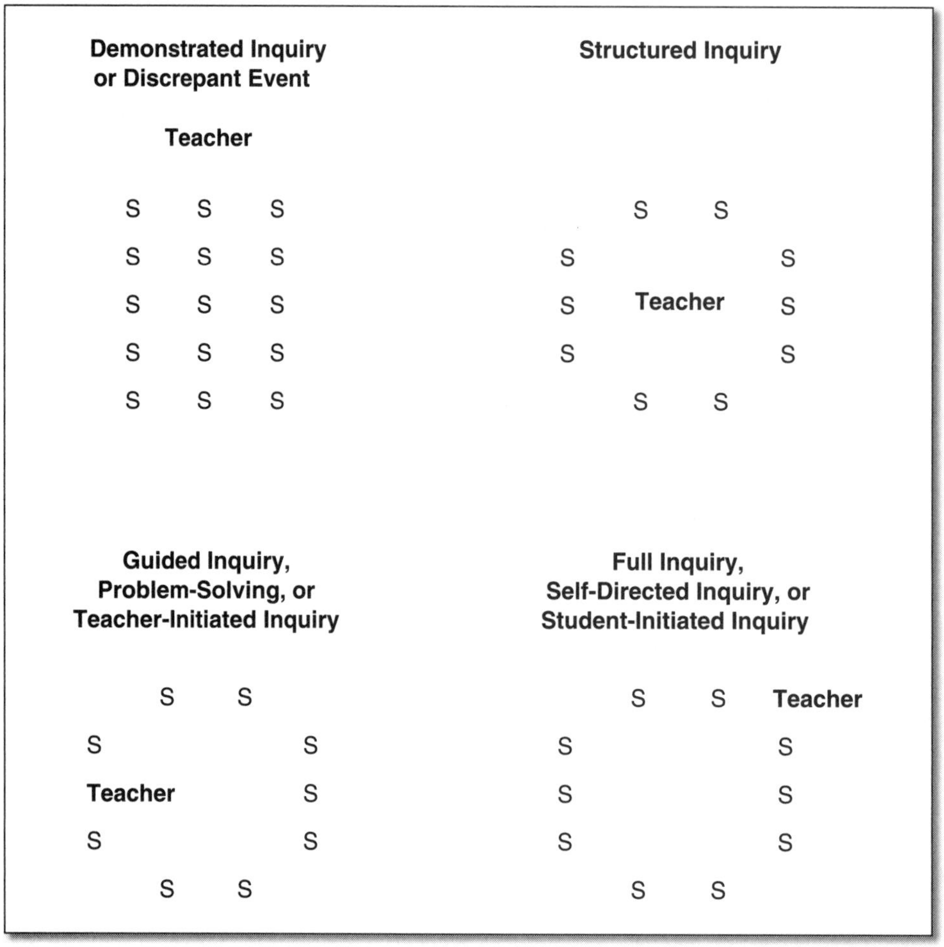

**Demonstrated Inquiry
or Discrepant Event**

Teacher

S	S	S
S	S	S
S	S	S
S	S	S
S	S	S

Structured Inquiry

S   S

S   ...   S

S   **Teacher**   S

S   ...   S

S   S

**Guided Inquiry,
Problem-Solving, or
Teacher-Initiated Inquiry**

S   S

S   ...   S

Teacher   S

S   S

S   S

**Full Inquiry,
Self-Directed Inquiry, or
Student-Initiated Inquiry**

S   S   **Teacher**

S   ...   S

S   ...   S

S   ...   S

S   S

Figure 1.7   Teacher Positions

During a structured inquiry, the teacher assumes the role as a *coach* and takes a position of "calling the directions" of the activity and having the students "play out" the procedure in small groups. The teacher maintains a central focus, but in this case, moves from group to group, assisting and clarifying the directions to students and critiquing their data and results.

During a guided inquiry, problem solving, or teacher-initiated inquiry approach, the teacher takes a less centered position and assumes the role of a *facilitator* or peer investigator—standing alongside the student groups. Similar to the structured activity, the teacher moves around to the individual groups providing guidance when asked but offers a less directed response to student queries. Here, the teacher may provide prompts and probing questions to help students decipher the question or problem being posed and suggests subtle responses that direct students to formulate their own procedures and explanations.

Finally, during a full or self-directed inquiry, the teacher takes on the role of a *mentor* without blatantly and overtly trying to influence the direction of the student or the small groups. In contrast to the "sage on the stage" during demonstrated inquiries, the teacher plays the role of the "guide on the side" in full inquiries. What this means is that as the teacher moves from direct instruction to inquiry-based instruction, she is astutely aware of her changing role and relationship with her students. Furthermore, as she moves from a dispenser of information to a catalyst for exploration and discovery, she becomes conscious of her physical stance within the classroom environment and understands how the shift in proximity to the students determines her style of interaction within the classroom.

ADVANTAGES AND BENEFITS
TO EACH APPROACH

There are several reasons teachers choose to demonstrate discrepant events, provide structured inquiries, give guided inquiries, or propose student-directed investigations. Each has its own advantage and benefit in an educator's instructional toolbox.

Demonstrated Inquiries and Discrepant Events

Besides being engaging and often entertaining, teachers choose to perform this approach when the following are present:

- The presentation results in a counterintuitive discrepancy from the observer's normal experience or acts as a cognitive hook to "wow" students and engage them in the upcoming topic.
- The presentation demonstrates specific skills and techniques for making observations and collecting data.
- The teacher wants all the students focused on a particular, controlled situation.
- Time, equipment, and/or supplies are limited.
- The content or topic is focused on a specific observable event or phenomenon.
- Toxic, flammable, or dangerous chemicals or materials are being used.
- An explosion may occur, and safety is an issue.
- The teacher needs to model a particular procedure.
- The procedure is complicated for students to follow.

Structured Inquiries

Likewise, teachers choose to perform structured, step-by-step inquiries or prescribed labs when the following are present:

- Students lack prior experience in self-directed learning.
- Specific skills and techniques for making observations and collecting data need to be followed.
- Time, equipment, and/or supplies are limited.
- The question and the results are predicated on a specific procedure to follow.
- Safety is an issue.

- Students need to follow a sequential procedure to obtain desired results.
- Students need to practice following directions.

Guided or Teacher-Initiated Inquiries

At the next level, teachers choose to give students guided or teacher-initiated inquiries, sometimes called problem-solving activities, when the following are present:

- The question or problem is focused, but there are many creative ways to answer the question or solve the problem.
- Teachers plan to give students choice and flexibility in solving problems.
- They guide students in how to map various ways to solve problems.
- They would like students to model the problem-solving process and appreciate and understand the ways scientists solve real-world problems.
- They want students to develop scientific reasoning skills in designing their own ways to collect, organize, and explain the results of their research.
- They want to emphasize attributes in decision making as well as habits of mind like creativity, imagination, persistence, and thoughtfulness.

Self-Directed or Open-Ended Inquiries

And finally, teachers choose to give students self-directed inquiries when the following are present:

- They want to give students choice and flexibility in posing their own questions and designing ways to answer those questions.
- They desire to have students model the process of inquiry and appreciate and understand the ways working scientists conduct investigations.
- They want students to design their own ways to collect, organize, and explain the results of their research.
- They want students to use scientific reasoning skills to explain the results of their investigation.
- And as in problem-solving situations, teachers want to emphasize attributes in decision making as well as habits of mind like creativity, diligence, innovation, and reflection.

Now that you have been introduced to the teacher behaviors and positions for each approach, go back to Figure 1.2 and compare the ownership modes to the behaviors (Figures 1.3–1.6) and positional stances (Figure 1.7) the teacher plays for inquiry approach. In doing this, you will embark on internalizing and articulating your involvement for each level of instruction.

You may also choose to take some time at this point to reflect on how often during the instructional year you presently spend on providing traditional demonstrations, discrepant events, cookbook or verification labs, structured inquiries, guided inquiries, and student-directed inquiries. Do you provide many more traditional demonstrations than labs and investigations? If so, what classroom conditions and restraints cause you to do this? How often do you plan for student-led explorations? Over the course of the entire school year, what's your present percentage of instructional time spent on traditional demonstrations, discrepant events, cookbook or verification labs, structured inquiries, guided inquiries, and student-directed inquiries? What would you like the distribution to look like a year from now? Three years from now? These questions should provoke you to reflect on your instructional delivery and plan the types of professional development you need to move from your present to your desired state of teaching.

WRITING QUESTIONS
FOR REFLECTION AND DISCUSSION

At the end of a chapter in many professional development books, the author provides questions for further discussion. Contrary to this and to model good inquiry, the questions should come from *you*. So whether you are reading this book alone, collaborating in a small study group, or participating in a college course or summer institute, write three questions you have. The questions may be about the challenge you face in implementing science inquiry in your school or a reaction to a section you read in Chapter 1. This exercise is designed to evoke thoughts, opinions, viewpoints, and, most of all, personal feelings about what you are reading. After you write your three questions, share them with others also reading this book. Set a few moments aside, maybe over coffee or pizza, to answer each question. Your questions, responses, and reflections will become beneficial as you progress on your journey into DSI.

Three questions I have include the following:

1.

2.

3.

The Art and Science of Inquiry

I once asked an art teacher how she teaches her students to paint. I asked the question because I felt there was an idiosyncratic similarity in how children learn to paint compared to how they learn to do science. During our conversation, Edwina, an experienced artist and teacher, explained, "In the beginning, children usually are introduced to art through finger painting." She described how children use their fingers and hands to explore different colors and combination of colors as they make an attempt to draw images and patterns. "Finger painting is a haptic experience," she illustrated, "that provides children with a rudimentary exposure to creativity and free expression. This visual encounter provides the opportunity for children to explore how colors mix together to form additional colors as well as how to create forms and images using a hands-on methodology."

Edwina suggested that the next step in teaching art might be to have the teacher draw an outline of a familiar object and have students fill in the outlines using crayons, colored pencils, or tempera paints. "Children are familiar with this type of learning. It is reinforced at home and school through the use of coloring books," she explained. Coloring books are very popular, and they provide the assistance young artists need. "The lines are your friends," she added, "so stay within the lines." A similar and well-known example of filling in the prescribed lines of a drawing is the "paint-by-numbers" painting popularized in the 1950s. With paint by numbers, the individual is given a background canvas or board with a dictated outline of an image or scene. Each outline contains a number corresponding to a particular premixed, numbered paint color. The child then uses a brush to fill in the outline with the identified paint color. The completed painting can make anybody look like a Rembrandt!

The next level of art instruction may involve the student joining a formalized class where the teacher places a bowl of fruit on a table and has each student in the class draw or paint the bowl and fruit. Some students may choose to paint the scene by using watercolors; others may use oil paints, acrylics, colored pencils, or pastels. In this situation, the students are given the task of drawing or painting a bowl of fruit but can choose his or her distinct representation of the bowl and fruit. In the end, many of the final artistic renditions may look similar, yet each has its distinctive interpretation of the image.

Finally, in the last level, students are asked to find their preferred entity to paint. For some, it might be a still life of more fruit; for others, it may be flowers, portraits, landscapes, seascapes, or abstract art. In any case, the choice of the subject and the medium of expression lies with the individual.

Now, let's see how this art example is analogous to how children learn to do science. As learning to be an artist may have started with finger painting, for many of us, our first experience with science may have started in the sandbox or even in the bathtub. It was a fun place to learn. We may not have known it, but in the sandbox, as we were scooping, pouring, and sifting, we were actually "experimenting" with the notion of heavier and lighter objects and the transfer of energy and matter. As we filled our pails with sand and made medieval sandcastles, we were actually experiencing opportunities for trial and error and learning lifelong skills like cooperating and sharing with others. If you cannot relate to being a sandbox scientist, then maybe the bathtub was your first opportunity to discover the principles of floating, sinking, and buoyancy. But I won't go into that here. You get the point. It's much like the finger painting example.

The next step of our formal introduction to science probably occurred during elementary and middle school where our teachers introduced us to the scientific method and doing "experiments." For many of us, following the step-by-step procedures of a prescribed activity or lab was the way we learned to do hands-on science in school. Just like paint-by-numbers "works of art" that end up looking somewhat all the same, so too were the results we produced from our science labs. In many ways, painting by numbers is just like completing structured, cookbook activities and labs. They both have an expected and predetermined outcome.

The next level of science, like the painting of a bowl of fruit, involves the presentation of problem solving and teacher-initiated inquiry tasks. In teacher-initiated inquiries, the problem is posed by the teacher, but the student is given the leeway to solve the question or problem in multiple forms. This allows a great deal of choice, ownership, and flexibility in completing the problem or task.

And finally, painting what you like is akin to student-initiated inquiries—where the relevant question or problem arises from the student's interest and curiosity. Just as the artist chooses her subject and medium of expression, the inquirer chooses his question and the means to attempt to answer the question. Therefore, open inquiry is a methodology for those who like to paint outside the lines! This author further contends that painting what interests a real artist is equivalent to the self-generated question that interests real scientists. Put in a contrasting light, painting by numbers is no more what real artists do than cookbook activities and verification labs are what real scientists do. But in too many elementary and secondary school classrooms, teachers "paint the picture" that science is following an orderly, step-by-step procedure. Nothing can be further from the truth!

TABLE 4.3 Alternative Assessment Formats

Concept Map

A concept map graphically shows meaningful relationships among scientific concepts. Students may be asked to generate maps without assistance or may be provided with a partial map to complete. Information about concept mapping and about software that supports the construction of concept maps can be found at the Concept Mapping Homepage (http://users.edte.utwente.nl/lanzing/cm_home.htm) and at a site sponsored by the Institute for Human and Machine Cognition in Pensacola, Florida (http://cmap.ihmc.us/Publications/ResearchPapers/TheoryCmaps/TheoryUnderlyingConceptMaps.htm).

Drawing

Drawing exercises are useful for assessing the knowledge of students for whom English is their second language and for students who find writing challenging. Drawing can be used to reveal students' knowledge before and after instruction. Seventh-grade students' before and after drawings show how their visit to Fermilab affected their understandings of scientists and the work they do (http://ed.fnal.gov/projects/scientists/).

Interview

An interview can be conducted with individuals or small groups of students and can center around a set of questions and constructs in advance or on the spot. Information about the interview as an assessment tool is available at the Alaska Department of Education and Early Development site (www.eed.state.ak.us/tls/Frameworks/mathsci/ms5_2as1.htm#interviews) as well as at the National Institute for Science Education's Field-Tested Learning Assessment Guide site (http://archive.wceruw.org/nise/).

Journal

A journal may include responses to questions given by the teacher, questions written by students that they wish to have answered, reactions to class activities and homework, or spontaneous reflections. Writing prompts keep journals from becoming diaries. Journals need to be read periodically if they are to be a useful assessment tool. More information about journal writing can be found at the online instructional strategies page of Saskatoon Public Schools' website (http://olc.spsd.sk.ca/DE/PD/instr/strats/journal/index.html).

KWL Chart

Originally conceived as a reading strategy, "KWL" stands for "What do you KNOW?" "What do you WANT to know?" and "What have you LEARNED?" Using a three-column chart, students are asked to write what they know about a topic in the left-hand column, what they what want to learn before instruction in the middle column, and what they learned after instruction in the right-hand column. Information about uses for the KWL chart, as well as examples, can be found at the Saskatoon Public Schools site (http://olc.spsd.sk.ca/DE/PD/instr/strats/kwl/) and at the site of ReadingQuest.org (www.readingquest.org/strat/kwl.html).

that in
re is an
student
art and
ure for
oncept.

Paint What You Like

Scientific Inquiry

of struc-
quire lit-
escribed
level of
toward
teacher-
like and
structure

This model leads us to the acceptance, appreciation, and understanding of the student's need for structure in the initial phases of learning how to inquire. Let's remind ourselves that effective modeling is a form of providing structure and guidance. And in fact, students need structure in developing science process skills and procedural knowledge, as well as formulating positive attitudes about the nature of science. In too many science classrooms, however, students have few opportunities to go beyond the step-by-step, procedural approaches to learning science unable to shed the shackles of structure and venture out to discover science on their own terms. Since science activities need to be more than the orderly orchestration of desired results, my advice to science teachers is to start teaching "outside the box."

DIRECTIVE AND SUPPORTIVE BEHAVIORS

Returning once again to the Invitation to Inquiry Grid, the four approaches provide different levels of adult assistance and scaffolding behaviors. As teachers, every day we provide varying degrees of both directive and supportive behaviors to students. Figure 2.2 shows how each of the four approaches employs a particular level of behaviors.

Instructional Approach	Demonstrated Inquiries and Discrepant Events	Structured Inquiries and Prescribed Activities	Guided and Teacher-Initiated Inquiries	Self-Directed and Student-Initiated Inquiries
Role of the teacher	Motivator	Coach	Facilitator	Mentor
Directive behavior	High Directive	Medium-High Directive	Medium-Low Directive	Low Directive
Supportive behavior	Low Supportive	Medium-Low Supportive	Medium-High Supportive	High Supportive

Figure 2.2 Directive and Supportive Behaviors

Directive behaviors include those where the teacher primarily engages in one-way communication, spells out directions for the student, tells the student what to do and how to complete the task, and closely supervises the performance of the student. Directive behaviors are very much associated with structure, control, and supervision. Directive behaviors include language like, "You should," "You're required to," "You must," and "You have to." Supportive behaviors, on the other hand, include those where the teacher engages in two-way communication, listens, and provides help and encouragement, facilitates interaction, and involves the student in decision making. Supportive behaviors are closely associated with listening, praising, and facilitating. Supportive behaviors include language like, "You might want to consider this," or "You might prefer to try that."

In science, teacher-led demonstrated inquiries are usually high in directive behaviors and low in support behaviors. Here, the teacher takes on the role of a *motivator*. With structured inquiries, the teacher assumes the role of *coach* and provides assistance that is medium high in directive and medium low in supportive behaviors. Problem solving and guided inquiries require medium-low directive and medium-high support behaviors from the teacher, acting in the *facilitator* role. Last, student-initiated and self-directed inquiries necessitate both low directive and high supporting behaviors from the teacher. Here, the teacher takes on the role of a *mentor*.

Now, go back to Figure 1.7 in Chapter 1. Look once again at the teacher's position for each of the four approaches to inquiry. For the demonstrated inquiry, add "Teacher as Motivator" to the illustration. Likewise, for the structured inquiry, add "Teacher as Coach." And for the guided inquiry and student-directed inquiry, add "Teacher as Facilitator" and "Teacher as Mentor," respectively.

Understanding the distinction between directive and supportive behaviors helps teachers articulate the differences in methodologies and the reasons why they provide different modes of instruction for different situations. In other words, Differentiated Science Instruction (DSI) teachers truly understand the meaning of "different strokes for different folks."

"Flowers Are Red" is a song written by Harry Chapin on his 1979 album, *Legends of the Lost and Found*. The song strikes a chord, especially for elementary school teachers, contrasting directive and supportive behaviors and what inquiry teaching is all about. You may choose to get a copy of the song to help construct your own meaning of differentiation.

The intent of this chapter is to help elementary, middle, and high school science teachers move beyond the continuous stream of structured-based teaching and consider differentiating their science lessons based on fluctuating and varying student needs for direction and regulation. As a result, educators will realize that there are times to provide teacher-led and highly structured activities, while there are other times to provide ill-structured activities with student-managed flexibility.

The next chapters will further explore the concept of DSI by explaining how to engage learners to be creative and sometimes paint outside the lines.

WRITING QUESTIONS
FOR REFLECTION AND DISCUSSION

As you did in Chapter 1, from the readings in Chapter 2, write three questions that concern you. Share and discuss your questions and responses with a colleague.

1.

2.

3.

Differentiated Science Inquiry

WHAT IS DIFFERENTIATED SCIENCE INQUIRY?

Chapter 1, "Pathways to Inquiry," implied a whole-class approach to inquiry. That means the teacher usually selects *one* inquiry approach for *all* the students in the class for a particular topic. In this chapter, we will be introduced to Differentiated Science Inquiry (DSI) and the various possibilities that combine a mixture of approaches to inquiry within the same lesson, thus offering different methods of inquiry for different student learning needs. Using a differentiated inquiry approach, the teacher constructs a science investigation with multiple or tired levels of guidance and structure so that each learner has an opportunity to choose a level that is developmentally appropriate for his or her particular learning style. Although the lesson offers various process-oriented pathways, in the end, all students arrive at the common understanding of the concept and standard being studied.

Although many of us are familiar with the various approaches to inquiry, DSI takes a slightly different twist. When used judiciously, DSI is an instructional practice that enhances classroom learning by matching the individual student's needs and learning style to the level of structured and guidance inherent in an inquiry lesson. In DSI, teachers recognize and value a student's particular learning style (or styles) as well as the student's need for guided instruction and structure versus less structured, open-ended learning opportunities. Teachers additionally provide need-satisfying environments on top of various levels of learning experiences and investigations based on student choice and tailored toward students' personal requisites. When teachers differentiate the approach or level of science inquiry, they do so in response to the child's readiness and preferred learning style—whether it is visual, auditory, tactile, or kinesthetic. Readiness and learning styles will be addressed in more detail later in Chapter 4.

ONE SIZE DOES NOT FIT ALL

Imagine a coach ordering jerseys for a middle school basketball team. The coach orders all medium-size jerseys, and when the jerseys arrive, passes them out during a practice session the day before the first game of the season. For most players, the jerseys fit fine. For others, the jerseys are either too big or too small. Mike plays the guard position on the team and is quite small in stature. His jersey reaches almost down to his knees. Mike expresses his embarrassment to the coach. The brusque coach replies, "Just tuck in your jersey. It will be fine. Quit complaining." Rudy, the center of the team, is five foot ten inches tall and can hardly pull the shirt up over his head. He too voices his disapproval to the coach, but the coach responds, "That's too bad. Wear it. I ordered only one size." The other players quietly giggle in ridicule.

Unfortunately, the jersey story is a lot like many classrooms where we see teachers teach by the "one size fits all" preponderate method—lecture to preteach vocabulary, followed by a discussion period to reinforce the content, followed by a verification lab to confirm the fitness of the content presented earlier. DSI teachers take a dissimilar tactic. They know that students respond best to a variety of instructional methods, so they adapt their approaches by selecting the appropriate level of instruction based on the topic being presented and needs of the class. That's not to say inquiry-based teachers don't lecture. They do. For inquiry-based teachers, lectures and formal presentations are designed to apply and reinforce experiences, not introduce them. Using the Invitation to Inquiry Grid, DSI teachers design their yearlong science plans to include an array of demonstrated inquiries, structured inquiries, guided inquiries, and self-directed inquiries, generally moving from more structured to less structured opportunities as the school year goes on. For many teachers, offering various modes of learning is a skillful and impressive instructional leap—especially when the offerings include a range from structured activities to true inquiry-based investigations where students formulate their own questions from an open-ended exploration, plan their own procedures, and choose the means to collect and organize their data.

In many ways, DSI is analogous to a golf bag full of clubs. You wouldn't expect an experienced golfer to have just one driver or, say, one putter in his bag. The golfer carries a variety of golf clubs, each suited for a different situation. Sometimes, he needs a driver for hitting the ball long distances, while other times he needs a sand wedge for lofting the ball out of a sand trap. Teaching with differentiated instructional tools is just the same. There's a saying that "when the only tool you have in your toolbox is a hammer, every problem looks like a nail."

As challenging as this venture is, differentiating science instruction takes inquiry-based instruction one step further. As you will now read, Balls and Ramps is presented in four different approaches: as a demonstrated inquiry, as a structured inquiry, as a guided inquiry, and as a self-directed inquiry. The four approaches offer students the opportunity to choose a mode that best fits their interest, preferred learning style, and individual comfort level with inquiry-based learning.

BALLS AND RAMPS: A DIFFERENTIATED SCIENCE INQUIRY LESSON

The inspiration for differentiated science inquiry originated, in part, from an e-mail I received from a sixth-grade science teacher at Williams Middle School. Ms. Soto (the names of the teacher and the school have been changed) participated in a summer collegial book study using *Inquire Within* and became intrigued by the notion of offering different modifications to the marble activity described in Chapter 6 (Llewellyn, 2007). Since she observed a broad span of inquiry skills and abilities in her students, the interest of differentiating the levels of inquiry instruction as well as moving from a single-approach methodology to a self-selecting, "multiple-choice" methodology appealed to Ms. Soto. We continued to communicate over the summer to refine the concept of differentiated science inquiry and planned the initial DSI lesson for Balls and Ramps in the fall of the upcoming school year. Since Ms. Soto was unfamiliar with many of the underlying principles with forces and motion, she took the next several months to read up on several National Science Teachers Association (NSTA) print resources, including *Forces and Motion: Stop Faking It!* (Robertson, 2002).

The purpose of the Balls and Ramps activity is to have students explore the concept of motion energy and investigate variables that affect the momentum of rolling objects. The inquiry aligns to the *National Science Education Standards* (NRC, 1996) for Grades 5 through 8. During this activity, students will do the following:

- Design and conduct a scientific investigation (p. 145).
- Develop descriptions, explanations, predictions, and models using explanations (p. 145).
- Think critically and logically to make the relationship between evidence and explanations (p. 145).
- In addition, as a result of this activity students will understand the following:
  - The motion of an object can be described by its position, direction, and speed (p. 154).
  - Unbalanced forces will cause changes in the speed of direction of an object's motion (p. 154).

Note: Although the activity was originally conceived as a middle school level, Balls and Ramps can easily be adapted for elementary and high school classes.

Let's now imagine you were invited to observe Ms. Soto's Balls and Ramps lesson and have just entered her sixth-grade science classroom at Williams Middle School. There are 24 students in the class; one teacher, Ms. Soto; and one student teacher, Mr. Balfour. Mr. Balfour is from a local university completing his coursework for teacher certification.

Prior to your arrival, Ms. Soto and Mr. Balfour set up the room to accommodate three learning stations, with a fourth station across the hall in a vacant room. Materials for each of the four stations were preplaced in clear plastic baggies. Materials include assorted small wooden blocks, several 12-inch grooved plastic rulers, assorted-size marbles and balls, several golf balls, measuring tapes, and plastic protractors. A full description and explanation of the Balls and Ramps lesson plan can be found in Resources A and B.

"Today, students," Ms. Soto commences the lesson, "we will begin to understand the concept of motion energy and investigate variables that affect the momentum of rolling objects. To do this, you can join any one of four groups to learn about these topics." She then describes to the class the procedure and the level of structure for each station, emphasizing that students have a choice in selecting a particular station. Ms. Soto knows that at first, students may choose a station based on which friends choose the same station. She knows that as she continues to provide further opportunities for choice, students will begin to select approaches that best fit their learning style rather than by their friends' choices.

Before students go to their chosen stations, Mr. Balfour explores students' prior conceptions about motion energy. He begins by saying to the students, "Being good scientists, tell me what you already know about rolling balls. Take out your science journals, open to the next clean page, and write down five things you know about rolling balls. After you are done, pair and share your statements with a partner. Compare and contrast your statements. See what similarities and differences you had with your partner. You will have five minutes to complete this portion of the lesson. Is everyone ready?" Seeing that everyone is eager to start, he says, "Okay, begin!"

While the students are busy writing their responses, Ms. Soto and Mr. Balfour walk around the room making themselves available for any questions that might arise. They frequently scan students' written responses for the possibility of identifying any prior naive conceptions students may have about motion or friction. After the students have had a chance to compare and contract their responses, Mr. Balfour passes out several yellow 3-inch by 3-inch Post-it Notes to each student and asks them to write their favorite response from the assignment on the Post-it Note. He then asks the students to come up to the front of the class, one at a time, and tape the Post-it Notes to the whiteboard (see Figure 3.1). The class reads each response and discusses the 24 responses.

Mr. Balfour uses the Post-it Notes to pre-assess students' previously held notions and understandings about motion energy. As he reads them silently to himself, he scans the statements for possible incomplete or misconceptions held by students. He makes a mental note of any conceptions that will need further attention later in the lesson. Next, he, with the assistance of the class members, organizes the notes into patterns and relationships to make meaning of their prior conception. Mr. Balfour constructs a concept map from the students' Post-it Notes and adds linking verbs to connect one idea to another. The end product results in a semantic web of interrelated words that represent the class's present understanding on motion and momentum.

Once the preassessment is complete, Ms. Soto and Mr. Balfour are ready to move on to describe the four stations in the lesson. Since Ms. Soto's science room is carpeted, most of the small groups will work on the floor rather than at table tops. The carpeted surface gives extra room for students to move about and limits the balls from rolling too far. The carpeted hallway can provide an overflow if the classroom becomes too crowded.

With all the stations properly identified, Ms. Soto invites the students to individually choose a station to go to. She explains that each station

Figure 3.1   Post-It Notes Preassessment

has a different learning approach and that each student can choose which station he or she prefers. Once the students assemble at their chosen stations, they are ready to explore the forces of motion.

THE FOUR STATIONS

Station A: As a Demonstrated Inquiry

Station A is set up in a separate room across the hall. At Station A, there is a demonstration table. Student desks are arranged in rows and columns. At Station A, Mr. Balfour will follow the procedures identified in Station B but present them via a teacher-led demonstrated inquiry. Mr. Balfour will present to the group the question to be investigated and the procedure to answer the question. But before he begins, Mr. Balfour will post the question on the front board and ask students to clarify the meaning of the question. He will also ask students to suggest how they might go about answering the question and propose a procedure to follow. He will then lead students into deciding what data need to be collected and how might we expect the outcome to be.

While conducting the demonstrated inquiry, he will call upon several students to assist him in the presentation but will provide a structure in guiding the students in recording and interpreting the data. The students will then use the results for the presentation to construct additional meaning to their already held conceptions of momentum.

The demonstrated inquiry, by design, is very teacher led. Mr. Balfour also has several "going further" questions and investigations he will pose to the group who chose Station A. These questions will serve as a springboard to engage the students in additional inquiries after the initial presentation is modeled. Several of Mr. Balfour's follow-up investigations include the following:

- What would happen if we used different-size marbles (small = 1/4", medium = 1/2", large = 3/4") in the investigation?
- How does the release point on the ruler affect the distance the marble will travel?
- How will the distance the marble travels be affected if the ramp (ruler) is shortened from 12 inches to 6 inches?

Station B: As a Structured Inquiry

In one corner of Ms. Soto's classroom, Station B is set up as a structured inquiry (see Figure 3.2). At this station, the question and the procedure will be provided by the teacher, but collecting the data and examining the results will be the responsibility of the students (see Resource B).

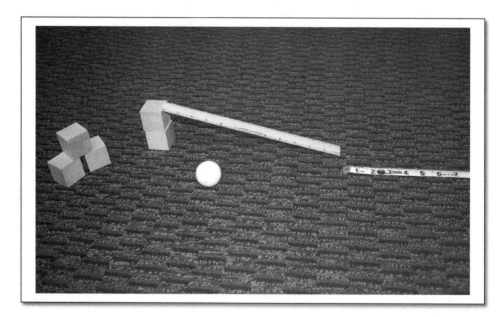

Figure 3.2   Station B

At Station B, along with the bag of materials, are several copies of directions available for the students who choose this approach. At Station B, students will write a statement or hypothesis to test, follow a given procedure, collect the data, but will determine on their own how to record and organize the data. Ms. Soto knows that some of her students may have trouble designing their own data table and explaining the results. For that reason, she has copies of a suggested data table (see Figure 3.3) to distribute if necessary. She knows that by giving the data table, she is providing more structure to the students who need it.

Balls and Ramps
Data Table for Station B

Title: _____

Height	Distance marble traveled			
	Trial 1	Trial 2	Trial 3	Average
1"				
2"				
3"				
4"				
5"				

Figure 3.3

Problem:

How does the height of an inclined plane affect the distance a marble will travel?

Materials:

One 12-inch ruler with groove

Five blocks (or books), each one inch high

Several marbles

One measuring tape

Graph paper

Procedure:

1. Place the 12-inch end of the ruler on the edge of a one-inch block.

2. Place the marble in the ruler's groove as far up the ruler as possible.

3. Release the marble.

4. Using that observation, make a prediction or hypothesis as to how the height of an inclined plane will affect the distance the marble travels. Record that statement in your science journal.

    My hypothesis: As the height of the ramp increases, the distance the marble travels will _____.

5. Repeat Steps 1 through 3 of the procedure for three separate trials. Using the measuring tape, measure the distance (in inches) the marble traveled for each trial.

6. In your journal, design a data table to record and organize the results.

7. Repeat the same procedure for two inches by placing a second block on top of the first. Place the ruler on the top of the second block so the height of the ruler is now at two inches. Release the marble and record your results in the data table.

8. Repeat the same procedure for three inches, four inches, and five inches, and again, record your results in the data table.

9. Calculate the average for each height. Show your work.

10. Use the graph paper to make a graph of your results. Be sure to provide a title to the graph and label the horizontal axis and vertical axes.

Conclusion:

Using the data collected, decide if the prediction you made was correct or not and explain why. Place your explanation on the lines below.

_____

_____

_____

Follow-Up Investigation:

In your science journal, design an investigation that will determine how the surface the marble rolls on affects the distance it will travel. Include a diagram to illustrate your design. Place the question being investigated on a sentence strip and post it above the area where you complete your investigation. Carry out your investigation and record all important data. Be prepared to provide an explanation as to whether or not your prediction or hypothesis was correct. Or you may choose to investigate any of the following questions:

- What would happen if we used different-size marbles (small = 1/4", medium = 1/2", large = 3/4") in the investigation?
- How does the release point on the ruler affect the distance the marble will travel?
- How will the distance the marble travels be affected if the ramp (ruler) is shortened from 12 inches to 6?

Similar to what students experience during the demonstrated inquiry, those who choose Station B will also be analyzing the data and evidence to seek patterns and relationship among the variables tested. Ms. Soto will be sure to question students about their drawn conclusion and what evidence they have to support their claims and conclusions. She will also ask students to form explanations and think about how they would communicate their new finding to others who did not do the inquiry.

Station C: As a Guided Inquiry

Station C is set up in another corner of the classroom. Station C is designed as a problem-solving activity or guided inquiry where the problem

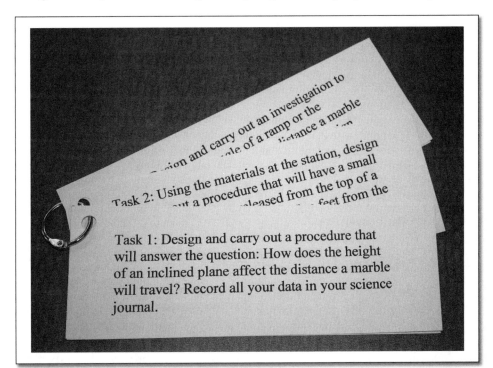

Figure 3.4 Station C Task Cards

task is provided by the teacher, but the procedure and collecting the results are left to the students. This station provides students with five laminated task cards and the materials to complete each task, although not all students will complete all five tasks (see Figure 3.4). There are assorted balls and marbles in the bag of materials that act as both distracters and enablers. In this case, rather than being told, students will have to determine which items they need (and which items they don't need) to complete the task. The additional materials may also spur other questions and tasks to investigate. On each card is a separate numbered task to complete.

Choose any one or more of the following tasks:

- Task 1: Design and carry out a procedure that will answer the question: How does the height of an inclined plane affect the distance a marble will travel? Record all your data in your science journal.
- Task 2: Using the materials at the station, design and carry out a procedure that will have a small ball or marble, when released from the top of a ramp, stop precisely at a point five feet from the end of the ramp. Draw an illustration of the design in your science journal.
- Task 3: Repeat Task 2, this time using a golf ball instead of a small ball or marble. Answer the question: How did you change the design of the procedure for Task 3? Record all your data in your science journal.
- Task 4: Design and carry out a procedure that will answer the question: How does the composition, diameter, or mass of a ball affect the distance it will travel? Record all your data in your science journal.
- Task 5: Design and carry out an investigation to determine how the angle of a ramp or the surface of the floor affects the distance a marble will travel. Draw an illustration of the design and record all your data in your science journal.

Include a diagram to illustrate your design. Place the question being investigated on a sentence strip and post it above the area where you complete your investigation. Carry out your investigation and record all important data. Be prepared to provide an explanation as to whether or not your prediction or hypothesis was correct.

At Station C, Ms. Soto will help students focus on a particular task and record a question pertaining to that specific task. She may ask these students to explain what data they expect to collect and how they will organize their data. At Station C, as students mark the end of their inquiries, she will prompt students into explaining the meaning of their results and their newly acquired knowledge.

Station D: As a Self-Directed Inquiry

Station D is set up as a self-directed inquiry. Here, students devise their own questions, design and carry out the procedures to solve the questions, and collect evidence to support or refute the claim or hypothesis made from the initial question posed. Like at Station C, there are assorted balls and marbles in the bag of materials that act as both distracters and enablers to complete the task (see Figure 3.5). Not all the supplies in the bag need to be used. Again, like Station C, students will have to determine

Figure 3.5 Station D Materials

which items they need to complete the task. The additional materials are expected to stimulate added questions to investigate.

The process for Station D mirrors the segments of inquiry identified in the Introduction. Students at Station D will first be directed to set up an exploration similar to the first two steps in Station B. From this initial observation, students will consider possible questions to investigate.

After reading all the possible questions, students will choose their first questions to investigate. Ms. Soto encourages students to record their question on sentence strips and post them on the wall above their work

Figure 3.6 Question on a Sentence Strip

area at Station D (see Figure 3.6). This way, every member of the group will be able to see what questions other students are considering.

If the group is large, several questions can be investigated at the same time. Each smaller group at Station D will seek additional evidence to propose a hypothesis or preliminary explanation. The groups then design their investigations to determine the variables and controls needed and design appropriate data tables to collect the evidence from their investigations.

Available at the teacher's desk are additional materials students might need in their investigations (see Figure 3.7). Materials include the following:

- Various-size groove ruler ramps (18", 12", and 6" lengths)
- Various-size wooden balls (1", 2", 3", and 4" diameters)
- Various one-inch-size balls (glass, wood, steel, plastic)
- Various-size marbles (small = 1/4", medium = 1/2", large = 3/4", extra large = 1")

Although each of the approaches has its own identity, all the stations demonstrate varying degrees of the seven segments of scientific inquiry introduced earlier. You can see as the approach become less teacher directed, the responsibility for the segments becomes more student owned. However, all four approaches will involve some aspect of analyzing the data and evidence, connecting new knowledge to preexisting knowledge, and communicating the results through whole-class discussion and reflection time.

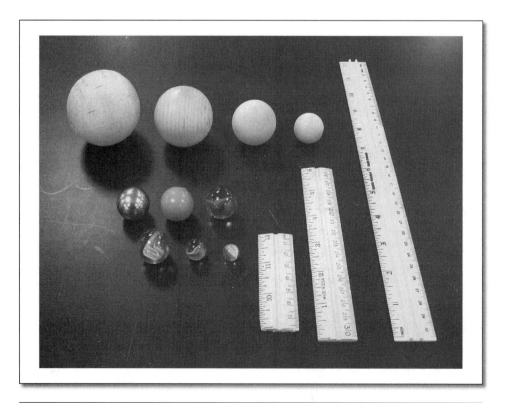

Figure 3.7 Materials Photo

VARIATIONS OF THE DSI MODEL

Balls and Ramps is just one example of how a teacher provided a way to differentiate the methodology for a lesson on motion energy. The example is provided with the understanding that most teachers may not have an additional teacher, adult, volunteer, or parent to present the demonstrated inquiry station. For many teachers, offering just three stations—B, C, and D—may be more suitable. Or for other teachers, only two stations are offered. Sometimes, based on the nature of the content, it is possible to present all four approaches. Other times, all four may not be applicable. The concept being introduced may lend itself to only two or three approaches. We will now identify six additional variations to this model and offer alternatives that may fit your class's needs.

The assignments or source for questions can fall into two categories: (a) those questions assigned by the teacher to all students and (b) those where the students have individual choice and self-assignment opportunities for the question. Usually, it is the teacher (or the textbook) who provides the assignment of the question and the method, not the students. Now, DSI can offer multiple options for both teachers *and* students. We will now look at several alternatives in assigning the question and method for the investigation, keeping in mind that different situations require different instructional responses.

Same Method Assigned for All Students

In this category, let's think of two teachers, Allen and Bruce, who use somewhat similar routines for teaching. Allen first provides an introductory lecture to preteach vocabulary didactically and then incorporates a conventional demonstration to illustrate the concepts made during the introductory presentation. In this case, Allen shows *all* the students in the class the *same* teacher-led demonstration. Later, Allen has *all* students carry out the *same* teacher-assigned, step-by-step, cookbook lab to reinforce what was presented earlier (see Figure 3.8).

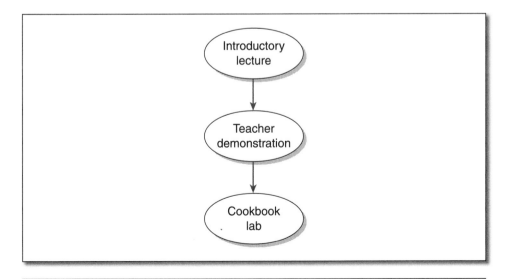

Figure 3.8 Allen offers the same assignment to all students.

Bruce also begins a lesson first with a lecture and then has *all* the students view the *same* demonstration. Following the demonstration, Bruce has students carry out the *same* structured inquiry or complete the *same* teacher-initiated, problem-solving challenge, or guided inquiry (see Figure 3.9).

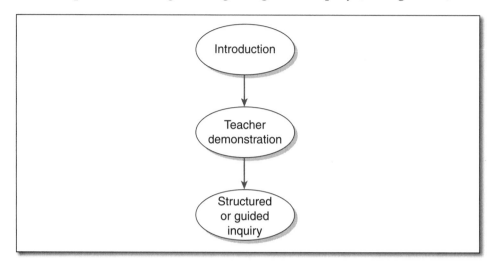

Figure 3.9   Like Allen, Bruce offers the same assignment to all students.

Due to preservice preparation and/or limited availability of resources, many science teachers fall into the "one-size-fits-all" style similar to Allen and Bruce. You may even have colleagues who are reminiscent of Allen and Bruce. And although these teachers may be highly qualified, successful educators, and their methodology may have a notable purpose, their teaching bears little or no sign of opportunities for student choice.

Methods With Opportunities for Choice

Now let's consider the next category of assignments. In this case, our third teacher, Charlie, provides both prescribed as well as nonprescribed methods, together with opportunities for choice. Charlie has *all* his students witness the *same* demonstrated inquiry but then makes an effort to offer students a *choice* of different follow-up structured activities and labs at least two or three times a semester (see Figure 3.10).

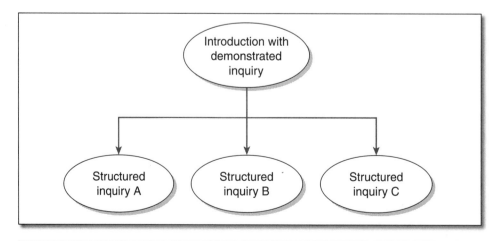

Figure 3.10   Charlie offers a choice of structured-inquiry assignments.

As an example, Charlie is presenting a lesson on the growing cycle of plants. To present this concept, he has his students grow bean plants under different lighting conditions: full light, partial light, and in full darkness. His students make daily measurements as to the effect of light on the growing bean plants. After the light experiment is completed and students make meaning of their results, he has students choose other variables to test as a follow-up investigation. Some students choose to investigate how the amount of water affects growing conditions. Others choose the effect of fertilizer or the type of light (white, blue, green, yellow, and red) in plant growth. Still other students design ways to determine if music affects plant growth, and if so, what kind of music promotes the most growth? In the follow-up investigations, the emphasis is on the self-selection of variables to investigate.

Our fourth teacher, Dave, is somewhat similar to Charlie. Dave has *all* students observe the *same* demonstrated inquiry followed by all completing the *same* structured activity but then offers students a *choice* in completing *different* follow-up guided inquiries and problem-solving challenges (see Figure 3.11).

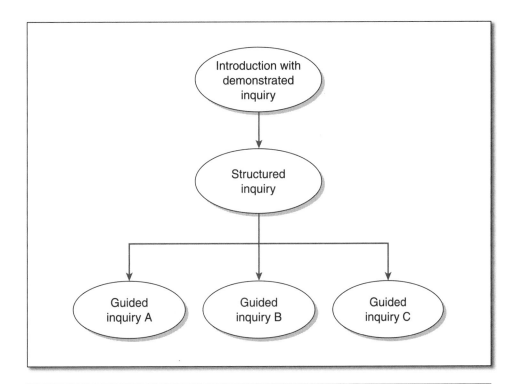

Figure 3.11   Dave offers a choice of guided-inquiry assignments.

Evan, our fifth teacher, is like Ms. Soto in the Balls and Ramps activity. He gives a brief introduction but then offers students a choice in selecting one of four different approaches that best fits their interests and learning styles. When differentiating science inquiry, Evan provides a bouillabaisse of activities—with each approach adding a taste of diversity, yet keeping it own distinct instructional flavor (see Figure 3.12).

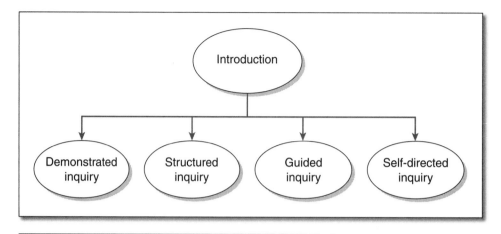

Figure 3.12 Evan offers a choice of four types of inquiry assignments in this instance, when he has another adult in the room.

If Evan did not have an extra adult in the room (like Ms. Soto had with Mr. Balfour), he might not have been able to offer the demonstrated inquiry option and therefore could provide only three stations: a structured inquiry station, a guided inquiry station, and a self-directed inquiry station (see Figure 3.13), making the analogy of this situation to a three-ring circus!

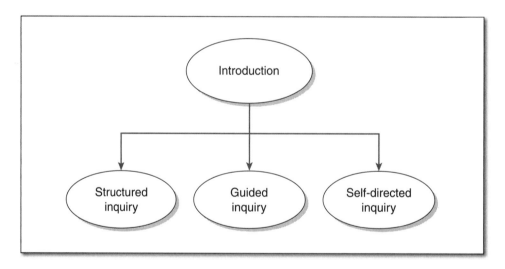

Figure 3.13 Evan offers a choice of three types of inquiry assigments in this instance, when he does not have another adult in the room.

As you can now see, there are many variations and possibilities for DSI. The range of approaches that best fits a situation depends on the teacher's tolerance for instructional diversity as well as the desire to attend to a variety of learning styles. It also depends on the nature of the topic, the sophistication and level of experience students have with science inquiry, as well as the teacher's professional goals and vision for science education. In actuality, teachers switch from one option to another when it is most appropriate. As you begin to implement DSI, you will come to acknowledge that distinctive instructional goals and objectives necessitate atypical approaches. A methodology for one concept may not work for another. Knowing what approach to use takes time and practice. Be patient and allow the appropriateness of methodology to germinate slowly.

THREE AREAS OF DIFFERENTIATION

According to Tomlinson (1999), there are three principal areas where teachers can differentiate in heterogeneous classrooms: content, process, and product. When differentiating content, the teacher considers *what* students are expected to learn. In this case, teachers may extend or further elaborate the subject matter for gifted and talented science students and for those needing an additional challenge, or on the other hand, provide academic intervention support in the form of corrective assistance where the content is complex or foreign to the student. When differentiating process, teachers modify *how* students will learn a new concept.

Using the Invitation to Inquiry Grid, the four modes of instruction provide the foundation for DSI. In appropriate and relevant situations, teachers can modify their favorite prescribed activities to provide varied levels of collaboration, challenge, and complexity. And finally, when differentiating products, teachers modify *ways* students can demonstrate what and how they learned. Students can exhibit their proficiency through standard assessment measures including multiple-choice and extended response questions, or through alternative or authentic means, including portfolios, journal entries, oral or PowerPoint presentations, performance assessments, tri-fold poster boards, and self-evaluations. Of the three areas just mentioned, this book will spotlight the *process* aspect of differentiation and provide instances when it is and isn't appropriate. If you would like to learn more about differentiating content, process, and products, there are a host of excellent books from Corwin. Two recommended resources are Gregory and Chapman's (2002) *Differentiated Instruction Strategies* and Gregory and Hammerman's (2008) *Differentiated Instructional Strategies for Science, Grades K Through 8.*

OTHER METHODS FOR DSI

Besides the variations you just read about, there are three other familiar instructional methods that support DSI: the K-W-L approach, the use of individual stations, and the 5E Learning Cycle. If you are already familiar with these three approaches, it's probably best to move on to the next section, Three Student Needs. If you are new or want to refresh your memory about K-W-L, individual learning stations, and the 5E's, this section is for you.

The K-W-L technique (Ogle, 1986) provides opportunities where students (1) assess their present knowledge of a topic, (2) raise and carry out their individual inquiries, and (3) elaborate on new knowledge gained. With K-W-L, the teacher begins a new unit of study by asking the class, "What do you already *know* about the topic?" During the K phase, students write their prior experiences on Post-it Notes or on a prepared K-W-L worksheet (see Figure 3.14). The teacher can collectively record the students' prior

K-W-L Chart

What do you *Know?*	What do you *Want* to know?	What have you *Learned?*

Figure 3.14

knowledge by listing the responses on the chalkboard or a large poster sheet under the "What I Know?" column. The teacher can also construct a concept map of the students' previously held knowledge and experiences and assess and uncover misconceptions students hold as they share what they already know about the topic.

Next, the students raise "I Wonder" questions and inquiries about the topic. At this time, the teacher or the students would record the questions in the "What I Want to Know" column of the K-W-L chart. If, however, students have difficulty writing questions to wonder about, the teacher can provide a nondirected experience in which students engage in an exploration about the topic of study. Exploring and observing an initiating engagement often acts as a prompt to stimulate questioning. The questions can now be listed in the "W" column and be discussed and reworded if necessary. The second part of the "What I Want to Know" stage involves students brainstorming ways to answer their questions. The teacher may decide to investigate one question for the entire class or allow two or three students to investigate their own question. As the students devise ways to solve their questions and go about carrying out their plans, the teacher rotates from group to group and encourages the groups to write down other questions that come up during the course of their investigations. Sufficient materials should be readily available at a supply center for groups to carry out their investigations.

At the conclusion of the "I Wonder" inquiries, the teacher and students record what they learned in the "What I Learned" column of the K-W-L chart. During this stage, the teacher helps students make meaning of their inquiries and make concluding claims and support and defend the claims based on the evidence collected. If a concept map was constructed during the initial "K" stage, the teacher and students can return to the concept map and add newly acquired knowledge to the map.

In many ways, teachers who implement the K-W-L strategy with small groups of students investigating their own question make accommodations for individual academic growth during the "I Wonder" portion of the strategy. Having six or seven individual inquiries going on in one classroom all at once takes years of practice and patience. It also takes flexibility and tolerance, but it can be done. Readers who want to know more about the K-W-L method will find a wealth of resources and strategies online and in academic libraries.

Likewise, learning stations provide occasions where students choose varying topics set up around the classroom in the form of individual discovery places. Learning stations can take many forms. They can be set up as individual exploratory centers for enrichment work or sequential stations where students choose a topic within a specified unit of study. Stations can also provide a means to assess students' understandings, skills, and abilities. "Measurement Stations" (Llewellyn, 2005), an article from *Science Scope*, provides 12 stations where students work in pairs to collect data from an initial exploratory task on the science process skill of measurement. Each station introduces the pair to a measurement skill with a step-by-step activity followed by "Inquiring Further" questions and tasks. When teachers allow students to choose the questions to investigate or choose the stations to explore, they make strides toward differentiating science instruction and enhancing self-directed learners.

The third method is the 5E Learning Cycle that was introduced earlier in the Introduction section of the book. Using the 5E's, Emily, a seventh-grade physical science teacher, integrates differentiated inquiry into her lesson as an adaptation of the Balls and Ramps activity. The first E, Engagement, commences the lesson with Emily assessing students' prior knowledge about rolling objects (much like Mr. Balfour did in the previous example). She then shows a quick demonstration of the ramp apparatus and how to release the marble at the desired height. For the second E, the Exploration phase, students complete a structured inquiry as prescribed in Station B. Following the Exploration, Emily leads a full-class discussion on potential and kinetic energy and lays the foundation for the district content standards for forces and motion during the third E, the Explanation phase. Then for the Elaboration or Extension phase, students choose one of the guided inquiry tasks as a follow-up investigation. Later, Emily provides time for students to communicate their findings and explanation for the investigations to the entire class during a "Momentum Convention." During this time, students engage in sharing their claims and supportive evidence. This phase of the lesson helps student to understand and appreciate the role of scientific argumentation as a critical means to how scientists enhance their knowledge about the natural world. For the final E, Evaluation, Emily prepares an appropriate unit test to assess students' understanding of motion energy as well as the elements in designing a scientific investigation.

THREE "STUDENT NEEDS" FOR DIFFERENTIATED INSTRUCTION

Like good teaching, effective differentiation centers on the needs of students. Tomlinson and Kalhfleisch (1998) remind us that if quality learning is to take place, regardless of the subject matter or method of presentation, three essential conditions need to occur. First, students need to feel emotionally safe, meaning free of intimidation regardless of their abilities or behaviors. Second, students need to experience an appropriate level of challenge, preferably just slightly beyond their ability and readiness. And third, students need time to reflect as *meaning-seekers* in constructing meaning from inside and outside of classroom environments and experiences.

In DSI, elementary, middle, and high school teachers meet the three criteria by valuing and recognizing a student's particular learning style (or styles) as well as the student's need for guided instruction and structure versus open-ended learning opportunities. The DSI-based teacher accomplishes this by providing various levels of opportunities and investigations that are built on student choice and tailored to students' personal needs by offering options and learning modes at different levels of challenge and difficulty. By providing a menu of choice and options, the student experiences what I call the "Goldilocks Effect"—choosing an activity that is not too structured or too open-ended—it's just right!

When a teacher differentiates the approach or level of science inquiry, she piques a student's interest in response to the learner's readiness, skill level, and preferred learning style—whether it is visual, auditory, tactile, or kinesthetic. Most of all, in DSI lessons, the teacher differentiates the instructional approach based on the student's attention span or need for structure, whether it is providing explicit versus ill-defined directions to a procedure or a traditional seating arrangement (rows and columns) versus a small-group setting. Furthermore, when a teacher differentiates the approach or level of science inquiry, she offers a variety of instructional practices that leads to students becoming more engaged and motivated in science classes. Creating opportunities for students to be appropriately challenged is predicated on designing activities focusing on choice, which leads to engagement, which leads to motivation, which leads to academic success.

With classrooms becoming increasingly academically and culturally diverse, teachers are challenged to meet these needs in all subject areas—but especially science, which lends itself to hands-on and manipulative learning opportunities. Differentiated inquiry can become the catalyst for flexible instruction and assessment, varied student groupings, variability in directive and supporting assistance, and acceptance for various routes for students to demonstrate what they now know and are able to do.

Although the reality of "teaching to the middle" and hoping to "reach as many students as possible" seems to be the predominate course of instruction in many classrooms, we now see there are instances where science teachers can differentiate an existing time-honored, favorite lesson and modify it to accommodate a range of learner needs.

The process of differentiation usually commences when teachers acknowledge the reality that classrooms are changing and that they need to reassess and recalibrate their instructional plans based on the varying prior knowledge, experiences, skill levels, and abilities of their students. In essence, there are two ways to deal with the changing climate of school classrooms: one is to ignore it and continue to teach to the "middle," knowing full well that many of our students will be either "lost" or bored, while the alternative is to make a resilient and passionate effort to adjust teaching to accommodate the various strengths and interests of the children and young adolescents entering into today's mixed-ability classrooms.

The naysayer may ask if the required planning is worth the time, while the risk-taking teacher unhesitatingly knows that best practices and various orientations to inquiry, when strategically employed, will maximize student engagement and achievement at every turn. In the end, DSI is not a panacea, and it's not the method "du jour." Understanding that all learning environments have their distinct physical and psychological obstacles, DSI is, however, an alternative means that teachers can employ once a month to shake up the ordinary routine of instruction. DSI can be an additional strategy teachers have in their instructional toolboxes to reposition learners from complacency to creativity.

WRITING QUESTIONS
FOR REFLECTION AND DISCUSSION

As you did in Chapters 1 and 2, from the readings in Chapter 3, write three questions that concern you at this point. Share and discuss your questions and responses with a colleague.

1.

2.

3.

If you are having difficulty writing three questions, consider the following guided questions for discussion and reflection:

1. Differentiating an inquiry lesson requires a substantial background in science content knowledge. What suggestions could you make to a third-year elementary school teacher who lacks a deep understanding in science but wants to attempt a DSI lesson?

2. What would you do if you planned three stations for an inquiry and the choices students made ended up in an unbalanced number at each station? For example: There are 22 students in the class, 15 choose the structured inquiry, 5 choose the guided inquiry, and 2 choose the self-directed inquiry.

3. Part of the "Communicating New Knowledge" segment involves encouraging students to critique and securitize the evidence presented in defense of claims made by others. How can you foster this skill without having the process become a shouting match?

4. Chapter 3 ended with identifying three areas where teachers can differentiate: content, process, and products. Choose a lesson or unit of study familiar to you. Describe how you could differentiate your lesson or unit for these three areas.

Why Teachers Differentiate Science Instruction

I n Chapter 3, we read how Differentiated Science Instruction (DSI) strives to have multiple options available for students to learn. As a flexible form of instruction, DSI creates opportunities for students to experience various facets of learning through inquiry in response to their distinct and diverse preferences. We will now address these learning preferences in more detail.

When choosing a model for instruction, which of the following factors most influences your decision?

a. The complexity of the task

b. The amount of classroom time available

c. Your preferred teaching style

d. The students' developmental level

If you chose "d," the students' developmental level, you are on the right track for differentiated teaching. Certainly, the complexity of the task, as well as the availability of time, are influential factors to consider, but putting students first is an essential element of DSI. If you chose "c" as your preferred teaching style, you may be putting your needs ahead of your students' needs.

DSI teachers plan units of studies according to their students' individual skills and abilities, preferred learning methods, and need for direction and supervision. Like snowflakes, they know each child is uniquely different. Teachers often use terms like *readiness, interests, learning style, tiered assignments, scaffolding,* and *flexible groupings* to accommodate these differences. It becomes necessary that any teacher developing the knack to differentiate inquiry lessons be able to articulate their understanding of the meaning as well as the mechanics of this form of instruction. Let's now turn our attention to briefly reviewing each of these terms.

READINESS

Readiness refers to a multifaceted array of a student's prior knowledge that determines his potential for achievement and success. We know that students come into our classrooms with different levels of knowledge, skills, and prior experiences and that these attributes have a profound effect on how children learn and interpret the language of teachers. The multiplicity of developmental factors affecting readiness can be influenced by language acquisition, reading and writing abilities, social status, cognitive capacities, reasoning skills, and physical and emotional dynamics. Nevertheless, when assessing a level of readiness, it is important to express the individual's competence in completing an activity as *task specific*—meaning that a student may have one level of readiness for Task A and a different level of readiness for Task B. The competence may depend on the nature of the activity, the interest the student has with the activity, as well as the prior experiences the student has with the activity. Therefore, labeling a level of readiness for a particular student from his performance based on Task X for all subsequent science opportunities should be unquestionably avoided.

Teachers can elicit students' prior knowledge and experiences on a new unit of study with the prompt, "Take out your science journals and write down five things you already know about _____." Students can then express familiarity with the new content through oral discussions, pair and share and word splash activities, or creating concept maps (see Chapter 3, Exploring Ice Hands, in *Inquire Within*, Llewellyn, 2007). The information gained will assist the teacher in matching the most appropriate inquiry approach with the student's level of readiness.

INTERESTS

When we speak of interests, we usually allude to the individual's zeal and desire that pique inquisitiveness for a particular phenomenon, both in and outside of the school setting. Interests can easily be assessed by administrating a numerical Likert-type science preference survey that asks students to identify topics of relevance and the preferred methodologies for studying those topics. For younger grades, a survey with smiley faces may be more suitable.

By administering a science preference survey in the beginning of the school year, especially on the first day of school, teachers communicate to students that individual interests and learning preferences play a vital role in designing classroom lessons and units of study. Figure 4.1 illustrates one example of a teacher-made science survey for elementary school grades.

For each statement that follows, fill in one "face" that best describes your response. Select ☺ for agree, ☺ for neutral, and ☹ for disagree.			
1. I like studying about plants and animals.	☺	☺	☹
2. I like studying about energy and matter.	☺	☺	☹
3. I like studying about the Earth and space.	☺	☺	☹
4. I prefer to make my own plans for a science experiment than to be given the steps by the teacher.	☺	☺	☹
5. I am good at following directions.	☺	☺	☹
6. I prefer to learn science by listening and reading rather than by doing activities.	☺	☺	☹
7. I like working alone more than in a group.	☺	☺	☹
8. I like to see how things work by taking them apart and putting them back together.	☺	☺	☹
9. I like to learn by watching others do it first.	☺	☺	☹
10. I like to draw pictures and models to explain my ideas.	☺	☺	☹
11. In science, I am more of a follower than a leader.	☺	☺	☹
12. I like to be told what to do and how to do it.	☺	☺	☹
13. I am good at designing experiments to do.	☺	☺	☹
14. I am good at organizing data and information.	☺	☺	☹
15. I don't like solving problems.	☺	☺	☹
16. I am good at seeing patterns and relationships.	☺	☺	☹
17. I like helping other kids who have problems understanding science.	☺	☺	☹
18. I am good at explaining my ideas.	☺	☺	☹
19. I am good at working in groups and cooperating with others.	☺	☺	☹
20. I like to learn by exploring and discovering.	☺	☺	☹

Figure 4.1   Preference Survey—Grades 3 Through 6

Figure 4.2 illustrates a preference survey that can be used or modified for secondary school grades. Both surveys are only models and suggestions. Any teacher choosing to use the surveys needs to add and subtract descriptors to suit his or her students. In some cases, students may need an explanation of the term. When analyzing the secondary school version, after the student completes the survey, add up the number of responses for each of the five individual columns. Record that number at the bottom of the appropriate column and determine frequency for the column with the greatest total. Although the results may not be totally "scientific," they can help students choose the appropriate investigation rather than the one their friends choose.

Structured	1	2	3	4	5	Unstructured
Follower	1	2	3	4	5	Explorer
Logical	1	2	3	4	5	Intuitive
Planned by others	1	2	3	4	5	Planned by me
Prefer clarity	1	2	3	4	5	Prefer vagueness
Prefer right answers	1	2	3	4	5	Prefer alternative answers
Task oriented	1	2	3	4	5	Idea oriented
Rule maker	1	2	3	4	5	Rule bender
Rational	1	2	3	4	5	Creative
Like order	1	2	3	4	5	Like flexibility
Specific	1	2	3	4	5	Diffuse
Follow given procedures	1	2	3	4	5	Make own procedures
Visual and/or auditory learner	1	2	3	4	5	Hands-on learner
Defined	1	2	3	4	5	Vague
Step-by-step	1	2	3	4	5	Trial and error
Prefer outlines	1	2	3	4	5	Prefer concept maps
Given answers	1	2	3	4	5	Find own answers
Like to be told	1	2	3	4	5	Like to choose
Like consistency	1	2	3	4	5	Like variability
Clear	1	2	3	4	5	Ambiguous

Figure 4.2   Preference Survey—Grades 9 Through 12

King-Shaver and Hunter (2003), Gregory and Chapman (2002), and Gregory and Hammerman (2008) offer other suggestions and examples for designing your own interest survey.

LEARNING STYLES

Learning style is the means one employs to acquire new knowledge and understandings. Basically, learning styles are identified into four types: visual, auditory, tactile (touch), and kinesthetic (movement). Although we may think of children (and adults too) as having one preferred learning style, most have multiple or combined styles that complement our individual personalities. Simply put, visual and auditory learners in your classroom may prefer more *expository*-like experiences such as visual demonstrations, readings, and minds-on discussions, whereas tactile and kinesthetic learners may prefer more *exploratory*-like experiences such as hands-on activities. Savvy teachers know that the best science lessons often integrate many learning styles.

Learning styles are also influenced by whether a child prefers more linear, sequential, step-by-step procedures versus systemic or holistic approaches. For middle school, many children still operate as concrete learners, while others are thinking in more formal or abstract terms. In addition, whether a child strives for individual competition versus group collaboration may also shape a learning profile.

Many readers may also be familiar with Howard Gardner's (1999) theory on Multiple Intelligences (MI). Briefly, Howard Gardner identified eight distinct intelligences:

- Verbal/Linguistic—those skilled in the spoken and written word
- Logical/Mathematical—those skilled in numbers, interpreting data, reasoning, and problem solving
- Visual/Spatial—those skilled in constructing mental and physical models, reading maps, as well as solving puzzles
- Bodily/Kinesthetic—those skilled in both fine and gross motor coordination
- Musical—those skilled in singing, playing a musical instrument, and composing music
- Interpersonal—those skilled in interacting and communicating with others
- Intrapersonal—those keenly aware of and who reflect upon their own emotions, feeling, and thoughts
- Naturalistic—those skilled in seeing patterns and relationships in the natural world

Since many readers are probably already familiar with Gardner's work, we will not delve deeply into his work. What we will recall is that according to Gardner, each of us has one or more dominant intelligences that profile our human intellect. And in fact, as he points out, humans probably have some degree of all eight intelligences. Teachers who embrace Gardner's ideas apply MI theory by designing lessons and assessments in which students can learn and demonstrate their learning through a variety of intelligences. Understanding multiple intelligences is one more way to become more aware of preferred learning styles. If you are not familiar with the work of Howard Gardner, there are numerous sites and references on the Web.

As a science teacher just starting to implement DSI, you may have your students identify a science inquiry approach based on their *perceived* learning style. A few years later, as you transition into DSI, you may want to develop a self-assessment of skills and interests for your students to complete and then use the results to help determine which approach best fits each individual. Later, as you become more proficient with DSI, you may want to more accurately assess your students' learning styles by researching and administering one of a variety of surveys and inventories to determine individual styles. Many examples are available on the Web by searching for "Learning Style Inventories." Several inventories include the 4MAT—Student Learning Preferences Survey, Silver Strong and Associates' Learning Inventory, and the Dunn and Dunn Learning-Styles Model.

With most science lessons, it is the teacher who determines how and when a particular approach to learning will occur. Under certain circumstances (and for good reasons) the teacher will decide that a demonstrated inquiry best fits the concept being presented. Other times, the teacher will decide that a structured inquiry lesson is best. We are beginning to see that in some cases, a lesson can be presented in more than one way—offering the student the choice to choose which approach best fits his or her preferred style of learning.

TIERED ASSIGNMENTS

In heterogeneous, diverse classrooms, learning opportunities can be modified based on the student's prior knowledge and experiences, as well as his or her level of readiness. Tiered assignments are designed to instruct students on comparable essential knowledge and skills but are provided at different levels of complexity, abstractness, and open-endedness. According to The Access Center (n.d.), tiered assignments help students to explore new concepts while promoting success and continued growth by providing opportunities that build upon one's eagerness to accept challenging, at-ability tasks. With tiered assignments, the curricular content and objectives are alike, but the process and/or the product are varied according to the student's developmental level, avoiding work that is neither anxiety producing nor boredom producing (The Access Center, n.d.). As King-Shaver and Hunter (2003) put it, with tiered assignments, "Students take different paths to reach common goals" (p. 76).

In the Balls and Ramps example, where the content standard calls for students to understand how "the motion of an object can be described by its position, direction of motion, and speed" (NRC, 1996, p. 134), some students may prefer to view a demonstrated inquiry, while others may choose to work in a small group following a prescribed procedure. Still others may want to be presented with a guided inquiry or challenge to solve, while many may decide to investigate the forces of motion through "trial and error" or experimentation. Implementing tiered assignments affords a fitting level of challenge for the student's attainment of success and fulfillment. Writing tiered assignments need not become a laborious task. At first, try adapting a single activity or lesson into a second alternative. Offer two options and later expand the choices as you become more comfortable managing multiple tasks concurrently.

SCAFFOLDING

When we speak of scaffolding, we refer to the level of explicit support and structure provided to students when completing a performance task embedded within the learning process. Like the scaffold alongside a building, an instructional scaffold supplies assistance to construct new knowledge. With strategic adult guidance and support, scaffolding helps a child move beyond her present level of development to perform at a higher level of skill and competence than she would have performed without such assistance. For many students, this kind of aid helps them to understand the concepts being explored. When students are left to explore on their own, as in an unguided inquiry or natural discovery approach, some may face obstacles and frustration, which inhibits their learning (NRC, 2007).

In Differentiated Science Inquiry (DSI), the teacher provides opportunities (in the form of various stations) for the child to perform at her current capability, but also offers additional opportunities (and stations) where she can progress into less structured and more self-determining and self-selecting modes. These scaffolding opportunities take the form of guided, semiguided, and independent methodologies and are translated into the four DSI approaches. At first, a student may choose a particular approach style (such as a structured inquiry) based upon his preferred learning, but progresses, with the assistance of the teacher, into more unconstrained inquiry-based forms of learning. In this way, the teacher purposefully diminishes or "fades" the scaffolding to enable the student to work beyond his proximal level of development (Vygotsky, 1978).

FLEXIBLE GROUPINGS

Not all students like to work collaboratively in groups. Some prefer to work autonomously and privately as individuals. Others are partial to working in pairs. Flexible groupings allow students to have a voice in selecting the group size in which they learn best. This includes a variety of individual and small-group settings, which, again, matches their needs and learning styles. Flexible groups may include both teacher-assigned and self-selected work groups depending on the following:

- The nature of the activity
- The amount of classroom time available
- The maturity of the class (or the individual)
- Which students can and cannot work together
- The extent of available supplies

Although student choice is a main contributor to motivation in inquiry settings, it is the teacher who is ultimately responsible for determining the size and configuration of the groups. As the antithesis to "tracking," where students are assigned to permanent groups based on their teacher-perceived skill level, children in flexible groupings are continually provided with different settings and learning contexts. In addition, the assignment, whether it is made by the teachers or the students, to a particular group is task specific. That means a child may choose to participate in one inquiry approach for one topic and another approach for a different topic. More specifically, Maria may choose to join the structured inquiry group for a topic she is unfamiliar with, say, topographic maps, while later choosing a self-directed group for a topic she is more familiar with, like the rock cycle.

The use of flexible grouping can also provide opportunities to work with individuals the student may not normally choose, allowing the teacher to assign groups on both a heterogeneous and homogeneous basis. Flexible grouping also lets the teacher assign group roles on a rotating basis to individual group members. In elementary schools, group roles and responsibilities usually include the leader, the recorder, the materials manager, the reporter, and the timekeeper.

As a word of caution, when students work in small groups (sizes of three or four), and you walk around the classroom to attend to the individual groups, observe the role each child plays in the group—especially when the group is mixed by gender. In groups where boys outnumber girls, you may often observe boys performing an inordinate extent of the manipulation of materials in addition to having the material located in their immediate accessibility. Girls, on the other hand, may be further away from the supplies being used resulting in limited accessibility. It's also important to be aware of who is controlling the direction of the activity. In mixed-gender groups, boys tend to "take over," while girls are assigned (or assume) the secretarial role of recording the data. Because boys tend to be more "pushy" and frequently presume a dominant role in the group, be sure all students have equal access to the materials and share the responsibilities equitably. Be equally observant when individual group members appear to have less status due to language ability, social ranking, peer acceptance, and interest in the topic being studied.

In the end, the purpose of flexible groups is to assure that all students, over the course of the school year, experience a variety of grouping arrangements (as well as varied individual roles and responsibilities within the small group) and that they encounter a diversity of working configurations based on their unique readiness, interest, and learning preference.

WRITING QUESTIONS
FOR REFLECTION AND DISCUSSION

As you did in previous chapters, from the readings in Chapter 4, write three questions that concern you at this point. Remember that self-initiated questions model good inquiry and lead you on to a pathway of reflection. When done, share and discuss your questions and responses with a colleague.

1.

2.

3.

Motivation—The Key to Unlock Learning

THE THINGS THAT MOVE US

Whether you are a parent, an athletic coach, a school administrator, or a classroom teacher, you know that providing motivation is crucial in fulfilling your role and responsibility as a leader. As science educators, conventional wisdom tells us that motivation is one key to student engagement and achieving academic success. "Nearly all educators," Jensen (1998) suggests, "deal with the issue of motivation. In fact, in the first few weeks of school, teachers often mentally group students into the categories of 'motivated' and 'unmotivated.' The rest of the school year usually plays out these early perceptions of who is 'ready to learn' and who isn't" (p. 62). Motivating individuals and overcoming student apathy has become the greatest challenge teachers, especially at the secondary level, face. As teachers, the contest lies in uncovering ways to engage those masquerading their complacency as "the uninterested" and "the underachievers" (Marshall, 2008). This is the assignment educators have been given since the age of the one-room schoolhouse.

I'm certain we all had a favorite teacher that motivated us. For me, it was Dr. Tik Liem (1987), author of *Invitations to Science Inquiry*. I would attend National Science Teachers Association (NSTA) conferences just to hear him speak. With credibility and humor, he demonstrated science principles by way of discrepant events, dazzling audiences with wit and showmanship. Now, think about someone who motivates you. Is it a former teacher? A role model? What is it about that person's character that gives you inspiration?

As teachers, we all want to motivate our students because we expect that motivated students lead to engaging classrooms and higher academic achievement. The purpose of this chapter is to understand the role motivation plays in creating engaging classroom lessons. This chapter will

(a) explain how choice encourages individuals to be motivated and (b) propose that in Differentiated Science Inquiry (DSI), students have an opportunity to choose which approach to explore a concept they wish to participate in, thus leading to greater commitment and involvement. The better we understand influences of motivation and choice, the better we are able to articulate why differentiated instruction makes a difference to the children and adolescents that walk into our classes each day.

We will begin by defining motivation as one's desire and willingness to engage in and successfully complete a task. Motivation activates goal-oriented behavior and gives one reason and direction in completing the task. For teachers, the task usually involves a particular aspect of the learning process. And although individuals may be equally and outwardly motivated to perform a task, the basis of their internal motivation may vary from one person to another (Lumsden, 1994).

Walk into any faculty lounge, and sooner or later, you will probably hear teachers commenting on the level of student apathy. Many will say motivation seems to wane as students progress through school. Teachers often cite how elementary school children appear to have high levels of motivation, while middle and high schoolers seem to be disenfranchised from school and its purpose. One teacher described it as "pretending to attend school."

Deci and Flaste (1995) ask, "Why is it that so many of today's students are unmotivated when it could not be more clear that they were born with a natural desire to learn?" (p. 19). Teachers often believe the answer to that question is that too many students try to get away with as little effort as possible. One middle school science teacher said, "Kids are more interested in iPods and texting on their BlackBerrys than they are in learning science." Unfortunately, that's probably true. So how do we motivate students to learn science? Understanding sources of motivation, both extrinsic and intrinsic, as well as the power of student choice, is fundamental to learning and the implementation of DSI.

EXTRINSIC MOTIVATION

Wlodkowski (1999) tells us, "Motivation is the natural human capacity to direct energy in pursuit of a goal" (p. 7). From your undergraduate educational psychology courses, you may recall that motivation is divided into two categories: extrinsic and intrinsic. Whereas extrinsic motivation focuses on the product or outcome, intrinsic motivation focuses on the process of personal accomplishment and enlightenment.

Extrinsic motivation involves completing a task in order to receive an external reward (or to escape punishment). It may also involve using rewards and reinforcements to solicit specific behaviors. Classroom examples of providing rewards include giving stars and stickers, candy, or other items an individual perceives as significant. Intrinsic motivation involves engaging and completing a task for its own enjoyment. Students who have internal motivation fulfill their own intellectual and personal needs through curiosity and individual interest. Deci and Flaste (1995) sum up the difference in motivation types as "having to" rather then "choosing to" (p. 5).

The behaviorist approach to learning, coupled with operant conditioning (using principles of reinforcement to obtain specific behaviors or desired results), has had a profound effect on teaching for the last 100 years. Teachers, as well as parents, who regularly employ external motivation strategies are often described, to some extent, as controlling, making the student's or child's behavior dependent on external contingencies and rewards (or punishments). External contingencies or reinforcements can take the form of a teacher providing a pizza party for a class performing at a desired level on a standardized test or a parent giving $10 for every A on a report card. Like the well-known carrot-on-a-stick strategy, rewards and incentives motivate through coercion and control.

As an external locus of control, using contingencies or reinforcements strikes a cause and effect between desired behaviors and outcomes. The use of bribes, behavior and/or performance contracts, and enticements, fortified with the fear of reprimands and retributions, are commonplace in classrooms and homes (Sullo, 2007). We often hear teachers using threats to control behavior by saying, "If you don't do this (or that), I'll put you on detention." A teacher who uses this language assumes the threat of punishment is an effective, long-range means to motivate a student to exhibit a desired behavior or change the student's actions. Erwin (2004) suggests there are categories in which people try to make other people do what they want them to do. They include the following:

- Asking and/or Pleading: "Would you *please* do this for me?"
- Telling and/or Yelling: "Just do what I say!"
- Bribing and/or Negotiating: "If you finish your homework, you'll get to go outside."
- Nagging and/or Criticizing: "Haven't you finished the assignment yet?"
- Threatening: "If you don't stop misbehaving, you'll be sent to the principal's office."

According to Alfie Kohn (1999), in *Punished by Rewards,* when teachers find students misbehaving in class, he suggests it takes effort and patience to explain respectfully to students the reasons *why* and *how* they should act appropriately. It takes talent and time to help them develop the skill of self-control and the commitment to behave responsibly. But it takes no effort, no patience, no talent, and no time to intimidate by saying, "Pay attention, or I'll pack on the homework." In this case, the threat of punishment becomes nothing more than an employment of power.

According to Sullo (2007), "Given that we've spent a century or so believing that external stimuli explain human behavior, teacher training programs typically require educators to learn how to systemically reward and punish students. Many educators thus see themselves as responsible for shaping the behavior of students by extrinsically rewarding them for compliance. Yet ironically, our system of rewarding students for academic achievement devalues the very thing we say we want: learning" (p. 5). It seems the only lesson *we* learn from this is that the more rewards we use today, the more rewards that we will need tomorrow.

This is not to say that extrinsic motivation strategies are ineffective. We just have to look at the salaries of professional sport players to see how money drives performance. Pay for performance is also a prevalent issue among educators. Some say merit pay will reward excellent teachers and rid the system of mediocrity. Yet most researchers say money is a short-term motivator and that a sense of belongingness and self-actualization are factors that truly motivate humans. I recall reading a story about a middle school principal who challenged her students that if they read 1,500 books over the summer, she would kiss a pig on the first day of school. As it turned out, the students met that challenge and read over 2,000 books that summer. The story made the six o'clock news, showing the principal "hamming it up" by putting lipstick on before kissing the pig on the auditorium stage for all the students to witness. In the auditorium, students howled with excitement as the event highlighted an emphasis on the importance of reading and the start of a new school year. Unfortunately, reward systems are short term and therefore to some extent fruitless over the long haul. The following summer, there was no reading challenge and the number of books read by the students dropped drastically. The moral of the story is that bribery works—but only for a short time.

I recently visited Marineland in Niagara Falls, Canada. It's a great place to observe conditioning and performance. One of the scheduled acts consisted of a group of dolphins doing tricks and jumping through hoops. It was a great show. The dolphins did their tricks and then received a reward treat. When the show ended and the trainer left, the dolphins stopped doing the tricks. The dolphins had no apparent interest in performing once the show was over and the rewards were gone. Whether we use the example of Marineland or the classroom behavior enticements, external reinforcements have a short-term effect.

Kohn (1999) suggests that rewards can be counterproductive. He says,

> To offer such an indictment is not to suggest that there is something wrong with most of the things used as rewards. It is not bubble gum itself that is the problem, nor money, nor love and attention. The rewards themselves are in some cases innocuous and in other case indispensable. What concerns me is the practice of using these things *as* rewards. To take what people want or need and offer it on a contingent basis in order to control how they act—this is where the trouble lies. Our attention is properly focused, in other words, not on "that" (the thing desired) but on the requirement that one must *do this in order to get* that. (p. 4)

There are certainly advantages and disadvantages of using rewards and punishments to control behavior. When overused, however, rewards and contingent reinforcements become ineffective, especially in classrooms. It is certainly not our desire to make our classrooms turn into replicas of mouse mazes and Skinner boxes. Stipek (2002) suggests that teachers should use extrinsic rewards sparingly and should make such rewards contingent upon the quality of a task or performance standard, rather than for simply engaging in, or completing, an assignment. That is to say, teachers should use rewards to acknowledge a job well done, rather than use rewards to control behavior. Giving out rewards for task completion can lead to superficial learning behaviors and less creativity (Ryan & Deci, 2000). Furthermore, extrinsic rewards undermine intrinsic motivation (Deci & Flaste, 1995) and fabricate behaviors dependent upon compensation or the avoidance of unwanted circumstances.

The challenge now, according to Deci and Flaste (1995), is not how teachers can motivate students through external incentives but rather how teachers can create conditions and environments in which students personally motivate themselves to increase the likelihood of their academic progress. Relationships between a teacher and a student that are centered on "You give me X, and I'll give you Y" are based on a transactional rapport. Relationships that build self-determination are said to be transformational. What kinds of transformational experiences can teachers provide to enhance intrinsic motivation and personal engagement in our classrooms? This will be answered in the next section.

INTRINSIC MOTIVATION

Intrinsically motivated learners have an instinct capability for competence and self-regulating behavior stemming from experiences that involve exploration of play, creativity, curiosity, and wonderment. When speaking of students being self-regulating learners, we think of students who control their own learning behaviors and demonstrate skills and abilities in the following:

- Self-planning
- Managing time effectively
- Designing and organizing procedures to follow in an investigation
- Designing procedures to accomplish a task
- Evaluating their own work through reflection

Providing students with opportunities to engage in open-ended science inquiry enhances their ability to regulate their own learning in three metacognitive strategies: planning, performing, and progressing. In planning, students analyze the task and identify the resources required for the performance. Planning also involves goal setting and planning for completion of the task. In performing, they act on the strategies designed to meet the task goal. Performing involves careful observation and note taking. As students carry out their plan, they act as self-regulating learners, exhibiting self-control and self-determination. Finally, in the progressing stage, students need instructional time for monitoring and modifying their progress through reflection and self-evaluation. Here, they can compare their performances against a classroom standard and make adaptive comments on how to improve their individual performance. While engaging in these three areas, students learn to take control of their own learning. They shift the focus of their work from teacher dependency to self-fulfillment and individual autonomy. But be mindful; this metacognitive process does not happen automatically. It is a process that takes quality time and needs to be taught explicitly as part of the expectations for an exemplary science program.

According to Stipek (2002), intrinsic motivation is based on the supposition that students are inherently motivated to develop their intellectual capacities and, in addition, take pleasure in their accomplishments—having feelings of self-fulfillment and enjoyment. Intrinsically motivated learners engage in noncoerced activities for their own volition—not because they have to but rather because they want to. Intrinsically motivated learners assert an internal versus an external locus of control. It is these innate internal motivational forces that stress autonomy and self-determination (Ryan & Deci, 2000).

We would all like our classes filled with intrinsically oriented students. Reality, however, finds us working in an atmosphere of packaged curricula, high-stakes testing, public accountability for content standards, overcrowded classrooms, limited resources, and pressures toward compliance—all factors that work against intrinsically motivated classrooms.

Alternatively, considering situations outside the classroom, many out-of-school activities are intrinsically motivating for elementary and middle school students. These include playing sports, joining church and community-related youth programs, as well as Boy or Girl Scouts troops. According to Ryan and Deci (2000), activities and situations that promote self-determination are intrinsically motivating and minimize feelings of being controlled. In a similar study, Hennessey (2000) found that activities supporting intrinsic motivation are also linked to high creativity. Studies by Tobias (1994) suggest that students who engage in intrinsically motivated activities demonstrate greater pleasure and persistence and increased confidence and participation. In short, they become self-regulating learners. When classroom teachers encourage students to pursue topics of self-interest and provide opportunities for self-direction, they become autonomy-supportive educators. According to Deci and Flaste (1995),

> What all this means is that being autonomy-supportive can be very difficult, especially with (students) who are accustomed to being controlled. Thus, [teachers] have to be patient; we have to work with our students to reawaken what is basic to their nature and what will almost surely lead where they are interested, and eager to take on challenges and responsibilities. We need to promote their autonomy, in part, by providing them with choice. (p. 149)

Let's now turn our attention to the bolstering student autonomy through the power of choice.

STUDENT CHOICE AS A MEANS TO INCREASE INTRINSIC MOTIVATION

As American citizens, choice is the backbone of our country. It is the foundation for freedom and liberty, protected by our Constitution and government. As consumers, we value the choice we have in shopping for everything from the food we eat to the clothes we wear. America's economy is founded on choice. Yet when we think about it, students have very little say about their schooling. Someone else, whether it's the state education department, the school district, or the teacher, usually decides what courses students will take, what content they will learn, when they will learn it, how they will learn it, and when and how they will be tested on what they learned. In most classes, students are told where to sit, who to work with, when they can talk, when they can have lunch, and when they can go to the bathroom (Guskey & Anderman, 2008). In many ways, schools have become an ideal lesson in instructional micromanagement.

In the Balls and Ramps activity from Chapter 3, students were given a choice in deciding which of four approaches best fit their individual needs and interests. Deci and Flaste (1995) report,

> The main thing about meaningful choice is that it engages willing-ness. It encourages people to fully endorse what they are doing; it pulls them into the activity and allows them to feel a greater sense of volition; it decreases alienation. When you provide people with choice, it leaves them feeling as if you are responsive to them as indi-viduals. And providing choice may very well lead to better, or more workable, solutions than the ones you would have imposed. (p. 34)

Although the research (Deci & Ryan, 1982) points to linkages between pro-viding choice and positively effecting intrinsic motivation, increased aca-demic performance, and persistence, teachers need to expect the unexpected as they provide more choice options in classrooms. This can be manifested in students choosing the easiest way out with the least amount of effort, claiming the assignment is boring, or saying, "I can't do this."

The teacher in the Balls and Ramps activity could have taken a differ-ent direction. Ms. Soto could have decided, as most teachers would have, to present the Balls and Ramps as a lockstep activity for the entire class to complete, regardless of her students' varied learning styles. Balls and Ramps, presented solely as a single-method activity, would have certainly engaged students in meaningful engagement and would have reinforced the use of many science process skills. Undoubtedly, the students would have most likely done what they were expected to do. Yet despite an amenable acquiescence to the completion of the task, we need to keep in mind that one student may experience frustration for the same task while another experiences joy and satisfaction. Again, one size doesn't fit all. Providing alternatives and choice is the key to DSI, enhancing the possi-bilities for increased levels of students' self-determination and self-efficacy. However, reality tells us that like any other instructional strategy, DSI is no "silver bullet." It is one more strategy that requires additional talent, time, and patience to scaffold the attitudes and behaviors of school-age youngsters into becoming independent, lifelong learners and building their self-efficacy.

According to Wlodkowski (1999), self-efficacy means, "Being able to organize and implement specific actions required for successful perfor-mance of a particular task" (p. 18). When a student first experiences an open-ended inquiry, she may raise a question of expectancy; in other words, she may probe her confidence regarding the likelihood that she will perform well on a particular task. She may ask herself, "Can I do this?" The question concerns an individual's judgment of her ability or capability to complete a specific performance. If a student has had prior success completing an inquiry task, repeated engagements in inquiry will promote increased competence and self-efficacy.

Similarly, Bandura (1997) says, "Self-efficacy refers to beliefs in one's capabilities to organize and execute the courses of action required to produce given attainments" (p. 3). And although *self-efficacy* and *self-esteem* are terms teachers often use interchangeably, they refer to two different concepts. "Self-efficacy is concerned with judgments about personal capabilities, self-esteem is concerned with judgments of self-worth" (Bandura, 1997, p. 11). When students demonstrate self-efficacy, they express persistence in completing a task, seeking help only after they have tried multiple alternatives on their own, and eagerly enjoying challenging tasks (Stipek, 2002). Certainly, science teachers will contend that their long-range goals for planning positive learning experiences include these behaviors—fostering both self-efficacy and self-confidence in their students. Studies indicate that a strong sense of efficacy fosters motivation and academic achievement. A student develops self-efficacy when he receives kudos, positive encouragement, and feedback from his teacher. Hearing praise like, "Good work, I knew you could do it" increases the student's confidence in completing a task.

CHOOSING A COMPATIBLE APPROACH

When choosing an approach compatible with one's learning style, the student may think the following:

- Does this task provide the support I need for successful completion?
- Is this task engaging, fun, or challenging to me?
- Is this task at my level of interest?
- Which task are my friends choosing?

Choice is the dragon slayer of complacency. Control versus choice, conformity versus creativity, and dependency versus autonomy are part of the everyday decisions teachers make in constructing the culture of their science classroom. It is an all-important value each of us brings to the classroom environment.

If research indicates that choice is such a powerful motivator, does that mean we give students the freedom to do whatever they want? Certainly not! They don't receive carte blanche. According to Deci and Flaste (1995), "Providing choice, in the broad sense of that term, is a central feature in supporting a person's autonomy" (p. 34). The challenge facing teachers is twofold: how to provide structure and guidance by setting limits without decreasing intrinsic motivation and how to provide opportunities where students choose within a range of options and utilize decision-making skills to foster personal learning.

Even in Ms. Soto's crowded science classroom of 24 students, inquiry-based science teachers can be autonomy supportive by providing opportunities for choice at both the individual and the group level, allowing children to choose paths that complement their readiness and individual learning styles or in the way they demonstrate what they know and what they are able to do at the conclusion of the lesson. Deci and Flaste (1995) put it best by stating,

> Part of being autonomy-supportive means allowing individuals within your class or work group to participate in making decisions about issues that concern only them, and part is sharing decision making with the group as a whole. The most effective, autonomy-supportive teachers allow their students (whether individually or as a group) to play a role in decision making. (p. 145)

Again, like any of the other science attributes mentioned earlier, helping students become effective decision makers takes quality instructional time—time that some will suggest can be better spent on teaching and reinforcing more content. Scaffolding students toward improved decision-making skills is a gradual evolving process. The question now is, "Are you willing to devote quality class time to develop opportunities for choice as well as the skill of decision making?" Teachers who answer, "Yes," find that some students may have initial trouble making choices. Providing opportunities for choice, however small they may be, allows students to develop proficiency in decision making according to their own idiosyncrasies. Examples include the following:

- Choice in deciding the number of members on a team or with who they will work within their group
- Choice in deciding the role and responsibility each will assume in a group
- Choice in deciding which variable to test in an investigation
- Choice in deciding how to collect and organize their data (rather than providing a data table)
- Choice in deciding how to communicate their findings and results to the class

Earlier in this chapter, you read how having a choice about the food we eat, the clothes we wear, or the music we listen to is a valued aspect of our culture. But for most adolescents and children, their choices are too often limited to beyond the classroom walls. The challenge to educators becomes the task of building empowerment and ownership within the school's instructional program.

THE CASE OF MR. MERRILL

In this case study (adapted from Deci & Flaste, 1995), Mr. Merrill, a seventh-grade science teacher at Red Wing Middle School, conducted action research in his own classroom as part of completing a master's degree in science education. Mr. Merrill wanted to determine under what circumstances his students may or may not want to make their own choices from one task to another. He furthermore wanted to know how he could encourage more autonomy and decision making in his science classes. He focused his study on his first two periods of Science 7. During Period 1, he had students work on measuring the dimensions of various wooden blocks over the course of several days. With Period 1 students, he was very directive and authoritarian, providing positive oral feedback for the number of objects correctly measured. With Period 2 students (who were similar to those in Period 1), he was less directive and more supportive. He provided nonjudgmental feedback as to the quality of the completion of objects correctly measured. At the end of the wooden block activity, he told both groups that they had an additional group of objects to measure. Mr. Merrill told the classes that they could either choose which objects *they* would like to measure or *he* could choose for them. The results indicated that Period 1 students, who experienced a more teacher-directed situation, overwhelmingly asked Mr. Merrill to select the objects, whereas the Period 2 students, who operated in a more autonomous situation, wanted to choose the objects for themselves.

Mr. Merrill concluded that one benefit of offering meaningful choice is that it engenders empowerment. Choice encouraged these middle school students to fully sanction what they were doing and allowed them to feel a greater sense of resolve. In his summary, he stated that he believed that all the students benefited from the measuring activity; however, the Period 1 students appeared dependent on the teacher, whereas the Period 2 students felt greater confidence in their measuring abilities as well their decision-making skills.

He also concluded that the goal of creating intrinsically motivated students seems best achieved when he was intrinsically motivated. When he is self-directed, trying new instructional methods, and demonstrating self-efficacy, he is more supportive of students' attempts at self-determination. Merrill's suggestion is supported by the work of Ashton (1990), who asserts that teacher efficacy has a consistent relationship to student achievement. In other words, when the teacher feels empowered, so do the children in the class.

APPLICATIONS TO DIFFERENTIATED SCIENCE INQUIRY

The challenge for inquiry-based teachers is to craft classrooms into more autonomous environments where students exercise self-regulating decisions about their learning. This, we have seen, is accomplished, in part, through differentiation and enacting opportunities for student choice. Thus, as teachers integrate inquiry-based methods into their science curricula, having alternative strategies, like differentiation, provides a scaffold that addresses the learning needs of all students. This means that while some students may need more direction and guidance from an adult, others are ready to move on to an open, self-directed science inquiry.

Subsequently, many studies tell us that choice is the corridor to autonomy. Autonomy leads to self-regulation and self-determination. Self-regulation and self-determination lead to self-motivation, personal empowerment, self-esteem, and expectably to increased achievement. It's a never-ending cycle that promotes autonomous learners to embrace an activity for the sake of the activity itself through curiosity and commitment. "If controlling people—that is, pressuring them to behave in a particular way—diminishes their feeling about self-determination, then giving them choices about how to behave ought to enhance them" (Deci & Flaste, 1995, p. 33). In the end, when science teachers provide opportunities for self-determination through choice, they demonstrate respect for the individual's academic growth—growth into becoming scientifically literate.

The onset of having students become scientifically literate citizens starts with teachers who can motivate and engage all learners. As teachers design meaningful instruction to enhance the willingness of the participants, according to the National Research Council (2007), they do so "by offering choice, providing meaningful tasks and an appropriate level of challenge, giving students authority over their learning while making sure their work can be examined by others, and making sure they have access to resources they will need to evaluate their claims and communicate them to others" (p. 203).

Similarly, White-McNulty, Patrikakou, and Weissberg (2005), from the Laboratory for Student Success at Temple University, sum up the motivation discussion by suggesting ways to foster a child's motivation to learn by focusing on the three C's: helping students to feel *capable, connected,* and in *control.* They suggest students feel *capable* when we hold them to high expectations, provide appropriate support and task-specific feedback, and focus on students' academic progress. We help them feel *connected* when we teach cooperation, encourage collaboration, and transfer responsibilities to working groups. And finally, we help them feel in *control* when we offer choices, teach decision making, make the curriculum relevant and interesting, and show the value of learning. The three C's add up to one essential aspect of motivation: ownership.

In closing Part I, you now have a better understanding of why teachers implement choice-based science inquiries to accommodate students' diverse interests and abilities. In Part II, we will see examples of how teachers put into action differentiated science lessons at the upper-elementary, middle, and high school levels.

WRITING QUESTIONS FOR REFLECTION AND DISCUSSION

As you did in previous chapters, from the readings in Chapter 5, write three questions that concern you at this point. Remember that self-initiated questions model good inquiry and lead you on to a pathway of reflection.

1.

2.

3.

However, if you would like several author-initiated questions, there are several provided below. Again, find time to share and discuss your questions and responses with a colleague.

1. What do you think the differences are between saying, "Students need structure," and saying, "Students need to be controlled"?

2. What evidence do teachers provide in defending their use of rewards and punishments in classrooms?

3. Some educators see classrooms as a dichotomy: those that advocate control of behavior or those that advocate permissive or laissez-faire environments. Where do you find yourself?

4. Are grades motivating to students? Make a claim and support it with research-based evidence and personal experience. Compare and contrast your ideas with a colleague.

5. Do rewards improve academic performance? Do rewards improve skilled performances? Make a claim to both questions. Support your claim with research-based evidence and personal experience, and then share your explanation with another.

6. Do you agree or disagree with the following statement? Rewards may change behavior temporarily, but they do not affect long-term attitudes and personal commitments. Provide a rationale for your answer.

7. Do you agree or disagree with the following statement? Children who are given rewards and punishments feel manipulated by another person in power. Provide a rationale for your answer.

Part II

The Mechanics of Inquiry—The "How" Chapters

Theory and practice are like two sides of the same coin. They provide the balance and synergy to fully grasp novel ideas and models. But ideas and models are somewhat futile unless they are contextualized into case studies that practitioners can actually use. Part II will do just that—guide readers into the practical applications of DSI with examples for upper-elementary, middle, and high school classrooms.

Leading off with Chapter 6, we will distinguish which activities are most appropriate for modifying a lab into a DSI lesson and which are not. Then, we will follow a straightforward process for adapting a traditional prescribed science activity or lab into the four DSI approaches. Next, Chapters 7 through 9 will provide examples of lessons with promising ways to present a science inquiry where self-selected choice and variability in structure are key elements. As you read through the examples, you will quickly realize that many of the lessons can be modified to a higher or lower grade level. Some of the lessons involve a minimal level of choice, while with others, choice plays a key role in the inquiry. Some of the lessons are based on the 5E Learning Cycle. Others are more straightforward. It also should be mentioned that each lesson needs to be supplemented with the appropriate content and vocabulary to fit your district and/or state learning standards.

How to Write a Differentiated Science Inquiry Lesson

SELECTING DSI ACTIVITIES

One of the first questions you are probably asking is: Which activities and labs are most appropriate for modifying? Often, activities and labs that contain multiple variables are the best to rework in a Differentiated Science Inquiry (DSI) format. In the Balls and Ramps investigation, there were several variables within the activity: the type of ball used, the mass of the ball or marble, the length of the ramp, the surface the ball traveled on, the angle of the ramp, the position on the ramp the ball or marble was released from, and the composition or density of the ball. Each of these variables can provide the basis for the initial investigation and subsequent follow-up investigations. As a life science example, if our initial activity is about growing seeds under different conditions, what variables may affect the germination rate of the seeds and the growth of the seedlings? You probably could mention the amount of moisture provided, the type of seed planted, the soil conditions, the amount of fertilizer provided, and the amount or type of light present during the early stages of growth. After providing an initial exploration, each of the additional variables becomes a source for succeeding inquiries.

With the Dropper Popper example (coming up in Chapter 9), students test whether or not the height at which a Dropper Popper is dropped affects the height the Popper rebounds. Variables that students can test include not only the height at which it is dropped but also the flexibility and temperature of the Popper, the surface the Popper is dropped on, and whether or not an added object is placed on the Popper when released. Again, these possible factors help to design the follow-up inquiries.

Not all science activities can be modified into the DSI format. Due to the natural immediacy of observable results, physical science topics may have a slight edge over life and earth science topics. That's not to say life and earth science topics can't be modified; they just take a bit more creativity and imagination. If you teach life or earth science, you need to understand that like many of your other activities and labs, they may need several periods to complete.

Let's take the situation of Mrs. Caster, a biology teacher at Ferndale High School. Each spring Mrs. Caster takes her eleventh-grade students on a field trip to a local pond for aquatic studies. She provides students with a choice of three different approaches to the pond study. In the first approach, she provides a step-by-step procedure for collecting, examining, and identifying collected specimens. In the second option, she provides a set of possible tasks from which students can choose to complete. In the third approach, she suggests that students first observe and explore the surrounding environment and then settle on a topic of interest and write a specific question to investigate. In this way, students are actively involved in choosing the topic and the means of investigating the pond community. Later, back in the classroom, all the students will report their findings and discoveries. Mrs. Castor will weave the student reports into a summary presentation on aquatic life that meets the district learning standards.

Labs with procedures that are flexible in design also make good activities to modify. This includes tasks where there is not just one sequential set of procedures for students to follow. A good example may be problem-solving tasks where there may be multiple solutions to a problem. If the procedure, however, needs to be carried out in a specific manner and sequence, the activity may not be best for students to design on their own. Chemistry labs, especially those where the procedure involves specific safety considerations, often fall into this category.

Start designing your DSI stations by first selecting a clear-cut, straightforward, confirmation-type lab. The lab should contain a question to investigate, a list of materials to use, a set of directions or procedures, a data table (with a grid to graph the data), and analysis questions at the end of the lab. This will become the basis for Station A, the demonstrated inquiry (if you decide to have one), and Station B, the structured inquiry. First, remove the data table and the grid from the lab sheet for Stations A and B. You may choose to have these available as separate handouts in case individual students get stuck and need assistance on designing their data table. But remember, in a structured inquiry, students should be encouraged to design their own data tables and the means to represent that data on a graph. Doing this helps them to understand and describe the relationship among the variables and later to effectively communicate their results and defend their explanations. Also, add a section at the end of the lab where students determine if their data are biased or flawed in any way. This will encourage careful analysis of the results and promote discussion. The Seven Segments, presented in the Introduction section, can guide you in incorporating all seven aspects of a science inquiry into Stations A and B.

Next, in Station C, the guided inquiry, students will be presented with an initiating exploration followed by several tasks to complete. Working individually or in small groups, students will choose one or more tasks and design a solution to solve each task. This is where the multiple variables come into play. Write your Station C tasks based on one of the several variables from the initial exploration. Again, in the Balls and Ramps exploration, the variables included the type of balls used, the mass of the balls, the length of the ramp, the surface the balls traveled on, the angle of the ramp, the position on the ramp the balls were released from, and the composition or density of the balls. Each of these variables can become a separate task for students to investigate in Station C.

For students who choose Station D, the self-directed inquiry, it is often necessary to first engage them with an open-ended exploration of the phenomenon. This will provide a context and a springboard for subsequent questions. Wording from the Balls and Ramps task consisted of, "Set up the materials as shown (provide an illustration or set of directions). Place the marble at the top of the ramp. Release the marble and observe what happens." This quick exploration will help trigger a number of questions to consider investigating. After completing the introductory exploration, students should be ready to focus on a question to solve. Follow-up directions may include, "Using the materials at the station, investigate the different factors (variables) that affect (blank) when (blank). In your science journal, write a specific claim for each investigation and collect and record the evidence to support or refute the claim made. Be ready to explain whether or not your claim was correct based on the evidence collected." Encourage students to write their investigative question on a sentence strip or separate sheet of paper and post it above their work area. Doing this allows you to quickly know what question is being investigated by the group, but most importantly, encourages the group members to clearly communicate the question being investigated. Students at Station D should also decide what data need to be collected and how they should be organized.

The modification process is actually quite simple. For the demonstrated and the structured inquiry stations, the directions are similar. You will then need to add several extension inquiries at the end of the demonstrated and the structured inquiries. For these, again look to the variables in the investigation to help design the follow-up inquiries. You may also use the same tasks from Station C for your extension investigations.

BALLOON ROCKETS

Balloon Rockets is an activity many are familiar with. It is one example of how an activity from *Invitations to Science Inquiry* (Liem, 1987) was modified into the four DSI stations. This investigation will yield a great deal of excitement but also require a good deal of classroom management.

The objective of the activity is to demonstrate Newton's Third Law of Motion—for every action there is an equal and opposite reaction. The activity correlates to the National Science Education Standards (NRC, 1996) for Grades 5 through 8:

- Unbalanced forces will cause change in the speed or direction of an object's motion (p. 154).

and the National Science Education Standards for Grades 9 through 12:

- Laws of motion are used to calculate precisely the effects of forces on the motion of objects (p. 179).

Each of the stations begins with an initiating event to engage the audience in observing and posing questions. Here are the four stations to Balloon Rockets.

As a Demonstrated Inquiry

Station A begins with a demonstrated inquiry and is followed up with an activity that can be presented as either another demonstrated inquiry or as a structured inquiry.

Materials:

- Several long, cylindrical balloons
- A spool of fishing line
- Plastic drinking straws
- Masking tape
- Measuring tape

Part 1 Question: How does a Balloon Rocket demonstrate Newton's Third Law of Motion (Action and Reaction)?

Procedure:

- Tie one end of the fishing line to a fixed point in the classroom.
- Select another fixed point about 15 to 20 feet away.
- Cut the fishing line at about 20 feet so it will reach the second fixed point.
- Thread the fishing line through one end of a drinking straw and out the other end.
- Tie the untied end of the line to another fixed point about 15 to 20 feet away. Be sure the line is tight and not sagging.
- Have one partner blow up a cylindrical balloon. Keep the open end (mouth) held closed. Do not tie the balloon shut.
- Bring the inflated balloon under the straw and tape the balloon to the straw. See Figure 6.1 below.

Figure 6.1 Balloon Rocket Photo

- Move the balloon to one end of the line so the opening is pointing in the opposite direction the balloon will go.
- Release the balloon and discuss what happens.
- How does the balloon rocket demonstrate action and reaction?

Part 2 Question: How does the amount of air blown into the balloon affect the distance the balloon will travel?

Procedure:

- Follow the directions from Part 1, but this time regulate the amount of air blown into the balloon.
- Have students write a prediction in their science journal as to what they think will happen.
- Identify the manipulated and responding variables in the experiment. Identify the factors to be controlled in the experiment.
- Use the table that follows (Figure 6.2) to record and organize the data collected.

	Trial 1	Trial 2	Trial 3	Average
1/4 Full				
1/2 Full				
3/4 Full				
Full				

Figure 6.2   Balloon Rocket Data Table

- Inflate the balloon one-fourth full. Keep the open end of the balloon held closed.
- Tape the balloon to the straw and release.
- Measure how far the balloon travels. Record the distance as Trial 1 in the data table.
- Repeat for two additional trials. Calculate the average for each inflation.
- Repeat the procedure for a balloon inflated one-half full, three-fourths full, and completely full, filling in the data table.
- Make a graph to summarize the results.
- Discuss the relationship among the variables.
- Discuss whether or not the students' predictions were correct.
- Form an explanation from the data collected.
- Connect the explanation to students' previously held knowledge.

As a Structured Inquiry

Station B begins with a structured inquiry and is followed up with a second structured inquiry and then a guided inquiry.

Materials:

- Several long cylindrical and several round balloons
- A spool of fishing line

- A spool of sewing thread, string, yarn, or other similar materials
- Plastic drinking straws
- Masking tape
- Measuring tape

Part 1 Question: How does a Balloon Rocket demonstrate Newton's Third Law of Motion (Action and Reaction)?

Procedure:

- Tie one end of the fishing line to a fixed point in the classroom.
- Select another fixed point about 15 to 20 feet away.
- Cut the fishing line at about 20 feet so it will reach the second fixed point.
- Thread the fishing line through one end of a drinking straw and out the other end.
- Tie the untied end of the line to another fixed point about 15 to 20 feet away. Be sure the line is tight and not sagging.
- Have one partner blow up a cylindrical balloon. Keep the open end (mouth) held closed. Do not tie the balloon shut.
- Bring the inflated balloon under the straw and tape the balloon to the straw. See Figure 6.1.
- Move the balloon to one end of the line so the opening is pointing in the opposite direction the balloon will go.
- Release the balloon and discuss what happens.
- How does the balloon rocket demonstrate action and reaction?

Part 2 Question: How does the amount of air blown into the balloon affect the distance the balloon will travel?

Procedure:

- Follow the directions from Part 1, but this time, regulate the amount of air blown into the balloon.
- Write a prediction in your science journal as to what you think will happen.
- Identify the manipulated and responding variables in the experiment. Identify the factors to be controlled in the experiment. Record these in your science journal.
- Design a table to record and organize the data you collect.
- Inflate the balloon one-fourth full. Keep the open end of the balloon held closed.
- Attach the balloon to the straw and release.
- Measure how far the balloon travels for Trial 1. Record the distance in your data table.
- Repeat for two additional trials. Calculate the average for each inflation.
- Repeat the procedure for a balloon inflated one-half full, three-fourths full, and completely full.
- Make a graph to summarize the results.
- Discuss the relationship among the variables.
- Discuss whether or not your prediction was correct.

Going Further Investigation:

- Design an investigation to determine how the type or texture of the line affects how far the balloon will travel. For the investigation, write the question being investigated on a sentence strip and post it above your work area. In your science journal, identify the manipulated variable and responding variable in the investigation. Make a prediction or hypothesis as to what you think will happen. Construct your own data table to organize the data collected. Be ready to communicate your results and form an explanation from the evidence collected.

As a Guided Inquiry

Station C begins with a structured inquiry and is followed up with a guided inquiry.

Materials:

- Several long cylindrical and several round balloons
- A spool of fishing line
- A spool of sewing thread, string, yarn, or other similar materials
- Plastic drinking straws
- Masking tape
- Measuring tape

Part 1 Question: How does a Balloon Rocket demonstrate Newton's Third Law of Motion (Action and Reaction)?

Procedure:

- Tie one end of the fishing line to a fixed point in the classroom.
- Select another fixed point about 15 to 20 feet away.
- Cut the fishing line at about 20 feet so it will reach the second fixed point.
- Thread the fishing line through one end of a drinking straw and out the other end.
- Tie the untied end of the line to another fixed point about 15 to 20 feet away. Be sure the line is tight and not sagging.
- Have one partner blow up a cylindrical balloon. Keep the open end (mouth) held closed. Do not tie the balloon shut.
- Bring the inflated balloon under the straw and tape the balloon to the straw. See Figure 6.1.
- Move the balloon to one end of the line so the opening is pointing in the opposite direction the balloon will go.
- Release the balloon and discuss what happens.
- How does the balloon rocket demonstrate action and reaction?

Part 2 Questions: Choose any of the following investigations to explore:

- How does the type and texture of the line affect how far the balloon will travel?
- How does the amount of air blown into the balloon affect the distance the balloon will travel?

- Inflate a balloon rocket that will stop approximately at 17 feet.
- How does the angle of the line (track) affect how far the balloon will travel?
- How far would the balloon travel if the line was completely vertical?

For each investigation, write the question being investigated on a sentence strip and post it above your work area. In your science journal, identify the manipulated variable and responding variable in the investigation. Make a prediction or hypothesis as to what you think will happen. Construct your own data table to organize the data collected. Be ready to communicate your results and form an explanation from the evidence collected as well as a description of the relationship among the variables.

As a Self-Directed Inquiry

Station D begins with a structured inquiry and is followed up with a self-directed inquiry.

Materials:

- Several long cylindrical and several round balloons
- A spool of fishing line
- A spool of sewing thread, string, yarn, or other similar materials
- Plastic drinking straws
- Masking tape
- Measuring tape

Part 1 Question: How does a Balloon Rocket demonstrate Newton's Third Law of Motion (Action and Reaction)?

Procedure:

- Tie one end of the fishing line to a fixed point in the classroom.
- Select another fixed point about 15 to 20 feet away.
- Cut the fishing line at about 20 feet so it will reach the second fixed point.
- Thread the fishing line through one end of a drinking straw and out the other end.
- Tie the untied end of the line to another fixed point about 15 to 20 feet away. Be sure the line is tight and not sagging.
- Have one partner blow up a cylindrical balloon. Keep the open end (mouth) held closed. Do not tie the balloon shut.
- Bring the inflated balloon under the straw and tape the balloon to the straw. See Figure 6.1.
- Move the balloon to one end of the line so the opening is pointing in the opposite direction the balloon will go.
- Release the balloon and discuss what happens.
- How does the balloon rocket demonstrate action and reaction?

Part 2 Task: Using the materials at the station, investigate the different factors (variables) that affect the distance a balloon rocket will travel when released along a line. For each investigation, write the question being investigated on a sentence strip and post it above your work area. Identify the manipulated variable and the responding variable. Include the factors, or controlled variables, held constant during the experiment. Include a prediction or hypothesis to your investigation as well as a data table. At the end of the investigation, include a description of the relationship among the variables and an explanation of your results. Be ready to explain whether or not your prediction was correct based on the evidence collected. Record all your notes and observations in your science journal.

BALLOON ROCKETS AS A 5E DSI LESSON

The Balloon Rockets activity can just as easily be modified into a 5E lesson having some aspects of all four inquiry approaches.

For the Engagement phase, the teacher can catch students' attention by blowing up a balloon and releasing it across the room. This will launch a discussion on the phenomenon of action and reaction. The teacher may also relate the balloon rocket to other action-reaction events.

For the Exploration phase, the Part 1 of Balloon Rockets will serve as a motivating opportunity to delve into Newton's Third Law. At the conclusion of the activity, all students should have a common experience to discuss balanced and unbalanced forces.

During the Explanation phase, the teacher will present a mini-lesson on Newton's Third Law of Motion (Action & Reaction) and explain why the air forcibly escaped from the balloon once the opening was released.

For the Extension phase, students will choose any of the Station C inquiries or complete a self-directed inquiry as outlined in Station D. The Extension phase will reinforce the understandings from the Exploration and Explanation phases and allow students to carryout their individual research.

Finally, in the Evaluation phase, the teacher will prepare an appropriate post-lesson test to assess student understanding of Newton's Third Law and knowledge gained from the lesson. The test should also assess students' understanding of designing a scientific investigation and controlling variables. The Evaluation phase should also include an assessment of the student's ability to communicate an understanding about scientific inquiry. See the *National Science Education Standards* (NRC, 1996), pages 148 and 176, for more details.

As soon as you read these few brief examples, you are probably saying to yourself, "DSI seems to take a lot more planning, preparation, and classroom setup time." Yes, at first it does. But soon after, you will begin to witness a renewed vigor of interest in your students that makes the additional preparation all worthwhile. For some, the challenges to a differentiated science inquiry lesson may seem more than you bargained for. For others, it can become a means to honor the diversity in learning and interest styles within your classroom. Only by accommodating the needs of our students do we effectively address the variability and range of students' abilities.

WRITING QUESTIONS
FOR REFLECTION AND DISCUSSION

As you did in previous chapters, from the readings in Chapter 6, write three questions that concern you at this point. Remember that self-initiated questions model good inquiry and lead you on to a pathway of reflection.

1.

2.

3.

Differentiated
Life Science Inquiries

The lessons in Chapters 7 through 9 provide a sampling of how teachers have modified their existing science activities and labs into a Differentiated Science Inquiry (DSI) format. Not all the lessons are complete, intentionally. What you will find are examples to guide you in modifying your own lessons and labs. Many, if not all, need additional content reinforcement to meet your district or state science learning standards. Some of the lessons are original. Others are taken from previously published resources. The lessons serve as a catalyst for your own creativity.

In this chapter, you will find two examples of differentiated life science inquiries. These are practical "how-to" experiences that will help you envision how you can apply differentiated science inquiries in your own situation.

WORM WATCHING—GRADES 6 THROUGH 8

Introduction: Children benefit from science lessons that provide concrete experiences through familiar materials. This life science lab has been modified from Sally Kneidel's (1993) *Creepy Crawlies and the Scientific Method.* In this activity, Mrs. Kelly's sixth-grade class will investigate the anatomical characteristics and the environmental preferences of earthworms (*Lumbricus terrestris*).

Estimated Time of Lesson: 5 to 7 days

Correlation: Worm Watching has been tailored into a 5E DSI format and aligns to the following National Science Education Standards (NRC, 1996):

- Living systems at all levels of organization demonstrate the complementary nature structure and function (p. 156).

- Reproduction is a characteristic of all living systems; because no individual organism lives forever, reproduction is essential to the continuation of every species (p. 157).
- Design and conduct a scientific investigation (p. 145).
- Use appropriate tools and techniques to gather, analyze, and interpret data (p. 145).
- Think critically and logically to make the relationship between evidence and explanations (p. 145).

Science skills: Observing, measuring, planning experiments, identifying variables, collecting data, analyzing results, communicating

Misconceptions: Some children may think earthworms are baby snakes. Others may have had previous negative experiences with worms, saying they are "yucky." Mrs. Kelly always has a small number of students that are initially hesitant to touch an earthworm. Most of their fears quickly vanish as the lesson proceeds.

Background Information: Earthworms are one of three types of "worms." One group of worms is the flatworms—which includes the parasitic tapeworm. The second group includes roundworms, many of which are parasitic. The third group is called segmented worms—of which the earthworm is a member. The earthworm has an anterior end (mouth) and a posterior end (anus). About one-third down the length of the worm is the "collar" or clitellum. This structure functions during reproduction where the sperm exchanges between worms. You can feel tiny hairlike bristles, called setae, along each side of the worm's exterior body. These setae help to hold the worm in place as it burrows through the soil.

Materials:

- Clean white napkins or paper towels
- Gummi Worms (one per student)
- Earthworms (one per student)
- Colored pencils or crayons
- Measuring devices
- Magnifying lenses
- Equal arm or triple-beam balances
- Water
- Plastic squeeze bottles containing water

Prior setup: Mrs. Kelly obtains Gummi Worms from a nearby candy store or the bulk food section of a supermarket. Live earthworms (or night crawlers) can be obtained by digging into the loamy soil where the worms live or by simply buying them from a local bait shop. She keeps the earthworms in a cool area in rich, slightly moist soil (potting soil without added fertilizer will do well) until the class is ready to use them. Adding some chopped-up, decomposed leaves to the soil will make the worms happy—at least until the lesson begins.

Day-by-Day Lessons

Day 1. In the Engagement stage, the teacher initiates the lesson by finding out what students already know about worms. A concept map of their initial understandings can be posted in the front of the room. Mrs. Kelly then introduces the objectives of the lesson and tells students they will be studying worms. Building up the anticipation of working with real worms, she brings out the candy worms to the "ohs and ahs" of the students. She places one Gummi Worm on a clean napkin for each student. Using magnifying lenses, the students observe the exterior of the candy worm. Using colored pencils or crayons, they draw pictures of the Gummi Worm in their science journals.

The following questions prompt students into describing the candy worm:

- How long is your Gummi Worm?
- How wide is your Gummi Worm?
- How much does the worm weigh?
- How many segments does your worm have?
- How can you tell the anterior (front) end from the posterior (back) end?
- What does your Gummi Worm feel like?
- What does it smell like?
- Can it be stretched?
- Can it be compressed?
- Are all the Gummi Worms exactly the same? How is your worm similar or different from other worms in the class?
- Make up a scientific name for your Gummi Worm (provide a genus and species).

Day 2. In the Exploration stage, the students follow a similar sequence of questions from the Engagement stage; only this time, they move from studying candy worms to real worms. To begin the Exploration portion of the lesson, the teacher first provides the proper procedures for handling live specimens—including washing hands before and after handing live animals. For more information about the use of animals in the classroom, see the National Science Teachers Association's position statement on "Responsible Use of Live Animals and Dissection in the Science Classroom" at http://www.nsta.org/about/positions/animals.aspx.

Students may also take part in defining the rules for handling the earthworms. The teacher should also instruct the students to keep the worm moist (using the plastic squeeze bottle of water) but not to have the worm drowning in water. Mrs. Kelly then distributes one earthworm to each student, placing the worm on a clean, moist paper towel. Similar to the Engagement stage, students observe the live earthworms and record the answers to the following questions in their science journal:

- What color is your earthworm? Using colored pencils or crayons, draw a picture of your earthworm in your journal.
- How long is your earthworm?

- How much does the earthworm weigh?
- Does the earthworm have legs? Eyes? Ears? A nose? Hair? A mouth?
- Is there a difference between the two ends of the earthworm? If so, describe the difference.
- What observations can you make to tell the anterior (front) end from the posterior (back) end?
- What does your worm feel like? If you rub your finger gently along the side of the worm, can you feel its bristles?

Days 3–5. Following the Exploration stage, the teacher now leads a full-class discussion to explain the science concepts and vocabulary related to the earthworm. The information may include the worm's scientific name, its habitat, its body parts, and a look at the worm's interior structures—including the digestive, circulatory, and reproductive systems. Students are always amazed that worms are hermaphrodites—containing both male and female sex organs. Mrs. Kelly has several nonfiction books available on earthworms to help identify the worm's physical features and body structures.

The differentiated aspect of learning occurs in the fourth E—the Extension stage. Here the teacher provides multiple inquiries in a station approach that students can individually choose to explore. The questions and tasks are posted on the wall so students can select which station they would like to investigate. The inquiry stations include the following:

- Design an experiment to find out whether earthworms prefer an environment that is light or dark.
- Design an experiment to find out whether earthworms prefer an environment that is dry or damp.
- Design an experiment to find out whether earthworms prefer an environment that is warm, room temperature, or cool.
- Design an experiment to find out what kinds of food earthworms prefer.
- Research how earthworms help aerate and renew soil conditions.
- Design an experiment to find out how fast earthworms move.
- Do earthworms react to different colors of light?
- What type(s) of soil do earthworms prefer?
- Or write your own question to investigate.

For each investigation, students will identify the manipulated and responding variables. They should include the factors, or controlled variables, held constant during the experiment and include a prediction or hypothesis to their individual or group investigation as well as a data table. Mrs. Kelly encourages the children to record all their notes, observations, and decisions in their science journal. At the end of each investigation, she prompts the students to include a description of the relationship among the variables and an explanation of their results. She encourages the class to use their collected data to look for patterns and relationship, form initial assumptions from the data, make more specific claims, and shore up those claims with supporting evidence.

Assessment: During the final E, the Evaluation stage, students prepare a poster board of their findings and explanations. Mrs. Kelly holds a

"Worm Convention" where each group has several minutes to share their discoveries about earthworms to the rest of the class. The lesson concludes with a summary of all the investigations and the new knowledge gained about earthworms. This new knowledge is added to the original concept map to visually show the new understandings constructed during the worm lessons.

Other Resources:

Terrarium Habitats by GEMS (Great Explorations in Math and Science, Lawrence Hall of Science, University of California, Berkeley, 1999).

INVESTIGATING PLANT GROWTH—GRADES 9 THROUGH 12

Introduction: In his book, *Biology Inquiries*, Martin Shields (2006) offers life science and biology teachers in Grades 7 through 12 laboratory experiences that can be effortlessly converted into structured and guided inquiries. In this lesson, *Investigating Plant Growth*, Mr. DiPorto's high school biology students use Wisconsin Fast Plants or Ward's Rapid Radishes to design a three- to four-week study of factors that affect plant growth and development. Fast-growing plants are especially suited to these types of inquiries due to their quick germination rate and hardy ability to withstand various classroom conditions. The lesson involves two parts. In Part 1, students will complete a structured lab to investigate the effect of varying amounts of fertilizer on plant growth. In Part 2, students then choose to complete either a guided inquiry or a self-directed inquiry. For the guided inquiry, several possible questions are suggested. For the self-directed inquiry, students will construct their own question and design a procedure to investigate the question.

Estimated Time of Lesson: Ongoing over a three- to four-week period.

Correlation: Investigating Plant Growth aligns to the following National Science Education Standards (NRC, 1996):

- Identify questions and concepts that guide scientific investigations (p. 175).
- Design and conduct scientific investigations (p. 175).
- Formulate and revise scientific explanations and models using logic and evidence (p. 175).
- Communicate and defend a scientific argument (p. 176).
- Organisms have behavioral responses to internal changes and external stimuli (p. 187).

Science Skills: Observing, measuring, planning experiments, identifying variables, collecting data, analyzing results, communicating

Misconceptions: Some high school students may believe that plant seeds need light and soil to germinate. Planting quick-growing seeds in a moist container filled with shredded paper or cotton balls and placing the container in a dark area may help to dispel the prior misconception. Encourage students to make daily observations and note that the seeds will begin to germinate in a dark area even without soil. Relate that when seeds are planted underground, there is little or no light. For information of student misconceptions about plants and germination, see *Uncovering Student Ideas in Science: 26 More Formative Assessment Probes, Vol. 2* by Keeley, Eberle, and Tugel. Arlington, VA: NSTA Press (2007).

Prior Setup: Mr. DiPorto provides a set of directions for a structured inquiry that focuses on a particular variable to test. The following tasks have been configured based on Shield's Investigating Plant Growth lab using Wisconsin Fast Plants. Wisconsin Fast Plants can be purchased through Carolina Biological Supply Company or Nasco Science. Rapid Radishes can be purchased through Ward's Natural Science. If Wisconsin Fast Plants or Ward's Rapid Radishes cannot be purchased, Mr. DiPorto can presoak lima bean or radish seeds overnight and then place them in a clear plastic bag to begin sprouting. The young seedlings can then be used a few days later for the student investigations.

The Lesson

On Day 1, Mr. DiPorto poses the question to the class, "How does the use of plant fertilizer affect plant growth?" He devotes 20 minutes of class time to generate a discussion to elicit students' understandings of the factors affecting germination and plant growth. After the discussion, Mr. DiPorto introduces a structured inquiry with directions and procedures. The remainder of the class period is used for students to receive the lab sheet, form small groups, and to read and discuss the investigation. Mr. DiPorto stresses that the students should talk over the investigation and be sure they completely understand what variables are being investigated and which are being controlled. He has the students clarify the question to be investigated and brainstorm what kinds of data the group will need to collect and organize in order to answer the question. Mr. DiPorto emphasizes that the students become "familiar" with the question before the investigation begins.

As Day 2 begins, students begin the fertilizer inquiry.

As a Structured Inquiry

Question: How does the use of plant fertilizer affect plant growth?

Materials:

- Fast-growing seeds
- Plant containers
- Potting soil
- Water
- Plant fertilizer (such as Miracle-Gro)
- Light source (if needed)

- Measuring spoons
- Measuring devices

Procedure:

- Fill four plant containers three-fourths full with potting soil.
- In each container, plant several fast-growing seeds about one-half inch below the surface of the soil.
- Devise a means to water each set of plants with varying amounts of plant fertilizer. For example: One set of plants will receive just water with no fertilizer; a second set of plants will receive a lesser amount of fertilizer as per the manufacturer's recommendation on the label; a third will receive the recommended amount of fertilizer; and the fourth set will receive more than the recommended amount of fertilizer.
- Label the containers accordingly.
- Decide how much water (and fertilizer) each plant will receive. Record all your decisions and data in your science journal.
- Design a data table to record the daily growth of all the plants.
- Each day for several weeks, observe, measure, and record the growth for all four containers.
- After several weeks, use the data from your data table to graph the results on a grid.
- Discuss the effect the varying amounts of fertilizer had on the growth rate of the plants.
- Make a claim based on the evidence and be prepared to communicate your findings to the entire class. The effectiveness of your presentation will be measured by how well you support your claim with data that substantiate your findings.

Once the students have their first inquiry under way, Mr. DiPorto introduces Part 2 of the lesson. In Part 2, students engage in a guided inquiry to investigate other factors affecting plant growth. Although students are conducting two experiments simultaneously, the structure provided from the procedure in the first inquiry helps to channel the design of the procedure for the guided inquiry. Mr. DiPorto also offers students an additional choice during Part 2 of the lab—to choose their own question to investigate and design their own procedure to answer the question. For Part 2, two-thirds of the students in the class choose to investigate one of the questions provided in the guided inquiry, while one-third of the students choose to complete a self-directed inquiry.

As a Guided Inquiry

Choose any one of the following questions to investigate:

- How does the color of the light affect plant growth?
- How does the amount or intensity of light affect plant growth?
- How does the quality or type of the soil affect plant growth?
- How does the amount of water affect plant growth?
- Does soothing sound (or music) affect plant growth?
- How do added chemicals (salt, sugar, lime, etc.) affect plant growth?

Materials:

- Fast-growing seeds
- Plant containers
- Potting soil
- Water
- Plant fertilizer (such as Miracle-Gro)
- Light sources
- Various colored acetate sheets
- Various types of soil (sand, clay, topsoil, gravel)
- Measuring spoons
- Measuring devices
- Sentence strips

Procedure:

For the investigation you choose, write the question on a sentence strip and tape it above the area where you conduct your investigation. Identify the manipulated and responding variables. Include the factors, or controlled variables, held constant during the experiment in your lab journal. Include a prediction or hypothesis to your investigation as well as a data table. Record all your observations, notations, and decisions in your lab journal. Make a graph of your results. At the end of the investigation include a description of the relationship among the variables and an explanation of your findings. Make a claim based upon the evidence and be prepared to communicate your results to the entire class.

This example shows how a teacher can "mix and match" various approaches to inquiry at the same time. Since plant growth is a gradual and timely process with some plant investigations, it is possible to have students engaged in two experiments at a time. Doing so encourages the elaboration of the botanical topic and the motivation of choosing. For some biology classes, having students conduct two experiments simultaneously may be too much for some of them to handle. For other classes, it provides a means for students to develop the skill of synchronized decision making and multitasking.

WRITING QUESTIONS
FOR REFLECTION AND DISCUSSION

From the two life science examples in Chapter 7, write three questions that concern you at this point. Share and discuss your questions and responses with a colleague.

1.

2.

3.

Differentiated Earth Science Inquiries

In this chapter, you will find two examples of differentiated earth science inquiries being applied in classrooms with elementary school and high school students. These are practical "how-to" experiences that will help you envision how you can apply differentiated earth science inquiries in your own classroom.

MINERAL DETECTIVES—
GRADES 3 THROUGH 5

The following vignette shows how Mr. Rob Schiller, a fifth-grade teacher at a mid-size suburban K–5 school, incorporates the varied interests of students, flexible groupings, and freedom of choice into a unit of study. Rob has been teaching for 10 years. In 2008, he enrolled in a summer science inquiry institute sponsored through a local university. Although new to science inquiry, Rob had previously developed several inquiry-based units in literacy and mathematics. He viewed the summer institute as an opportunity to extend his expertise beyond language arts and math and into science.

His district's fifth-grade science curriculum calls for a unit on "minerals." In previous years, his mineral unit centered on the school's "Rocks and Minerals" kit from Delta Science Modules. Delta is an excellent resource for elementary and middle school science teachers, especially for those interested in teaching hands-on and inquiry-based lessons.

Since Rob already had experience teaching about minerals, he thought he would apply his newly acquired inquiry-based science instruction knowledge and skills to planning the upcoming year's mineralogy unit.

As Rob looked through the Delta Kit's Teacher's Guide and studied the sequence of the suggested lessons, he saw an investigative-like pattern to the kit's activities. Many of them focused on testing a sample mineral for a particular property. The activities were designed to encourage students to observe and record data, and then identify the name of the unknown mineral, in a process, Rob thought, similar to a mystery investigation. Since many of his students are familiar with the television show *CSI*, the idea of having his 24 fifth graders become mineral detectives sounded like a challenging idea.

Rob next decided to search the Web and see what ideas and resources he could find. He quickly came across an article in *Science Activities* by Thompson and Carmack (2007) that helped him not only develop the unit's theme around detective investigations but also integrate language arts into the unit as well. Rob decided this would be a perfect opportunity to include the district's recommended reading of *The Adventures of Sherlock Holmes* into the mineral unit.

Rob's lesson plan demonstrates how he took "baby steps" to incorporate aspects of student interests, flexible groupings, and choice into an inquiry-based 5E Learning Cycle format. Let's examine Rob's first attempt at an inquiry-based science lesson.

Mineral Detectives Lesson Plan

Introduction: In this unit, students will observe and describe various properties of common minerals, recognize that minerals have certain characteristic properties, and conduct a series of tests on an unknown mineral to determine its name and use. In addition, Mr. Schiller will introduce vocabulary terms such as *geology, mineral, property, luster, metallic, non-metallic, hardness, streak, acid,* and *texture* to the students.

Estimated Time: Six 45-minute periods

Correlation With the National Science Education Standards (NRC, 1996):
As a result of this activity, all students will be able to do the following:

- Use appropriate tools and techniques to gather, analyze, and interpret data (p. 145).
- Develop descriptions, explanations, predictions, and models using explanations (p. 145).
- Think critically and logically to make the relationship between evidence and explanations (p. 145).
- Identify a substance by its characteristic properties (p. 154).

Science Skills: Observing, comparing and contrasting, classifying, measuring, communicating, collecting, reporting and interpreting data, inferring, hypothesizing, using models

Background: In this six-day unit, students will incorporate science process and inquiry skills to discover the identifiable properties of minerals. During the lesson, they will learn that properties such as color, luster, hardness, texture, and reaction to acid help distinguish one mineral from another.

Misconceptions: Most fifth-grade students may have limited experience with observing minerals and recognizing their names. They may confuse minerals and rocks and use the terms interchangeably. Early in the lesson, Mr. Schiller will pass around several examples of rocks and minerals. Students will use magnifying glasses to compare and contrast the samples and record their observations in their science journals. Later, constructing a Venn diagram will help students distinguish rocks from minerals.

Materials:

- Three sets of 10 assorted minerals (quartz, feldspar, mica, calcite, halite, talc, galena, pyrite, copper sulfide, sulfur)
- Magnifying lenses
- Plastic squeeze bottles of vinegar (dilute acetic acid)
- Steel nails
- Glass plates
- Copper pennies
- Mohs Scale of Hardness charts
- Streak plates
- Safety goggles
- Science journals

Safety Concerns: Mr. Schiller requires that students wear safety goggles at the acid test station and students wash their hands after using the acid bottles. Also, he covered the station tabletops with newspapers in the event of spillage or accidents.

Grouping Arrangements: Students will work individually or in groups of two.

Preparation and Prior Setup: Using shoeboxes and small plastic containers, Rob arranges the testing materials for each property into four stations: luster, hardness, streak test, and acid test. Each station needs one box of testing materials. Safety eye protection is required when testing the minerals with the vinegar (acetic acid). He also creates task cards for each station for students to follow when testing the particular property.

Day-by-Day Lessons

Day 1—Engagement Stage

To lead off the Mineral Detectives unit, Mr. Schiller poses a question to his class: "What chemical and physical properties do scientists use to identify and describe various minerals?" He writes the question on a sentence strip and posts it on the front board. Rob gives the students plenty of time to brainstorm their ideas and share their thoughts with the rest of the class as he silently assesses students' prior knowledge about minerals.

From identical sets of minerals, each student chooses one of 10 minerals in the set to "detect." The students next use magnifying glasses to observe color and other observable properties of their mineral and record the properties in their science journals. As the first day's science lesson comes to a close, for homework, the teacher tells the students to research other tests that can be done to distinguish one mineral from another.

Day 2—Exploration Stage

Day 2's science class begins with a whole-class discussion regarding the ways Mr. Schiller's fifth-grade detectives found to test minerals. Rob uses that information to transition the day's lesson into introducing the four stations that will test each mineral for observable properties (luster, hardness, streak, and reaction to acid). Next, he instructs students to design a data table in their science journals to organize their results for each test.

Mr. Schiller then demonstrates the proper procedure for testing minerals using vinegar and shows the correct safety procedures for wearing eye goggles during the acid test. One station at a time, students will now follow the directions on the laminated task card at the station and test their mineral sample and record the results of the test in their data table.

Day 3—Explanation Stage

On Day 3, using their data tables from their science journals, the class reviews the results of the station tests and identifies the chemical and physical properties of all 10 minerals tested. With each detective having his or her own test results, Mr. Schiller now directs each student to find someone in the class who has the same test results. Students with the same (or similar) results now pair up to find out the name of their mineral specimen using the Mineral Identification Sheet (Figure 8.1).

The students work together in pairs (based on the mineral they tested) to find the mineral's common name. As a follow-up homework assignment, the pair of detectives has to find a country or place where their mystery mineral can be naturally found and identify its use in business and industry.

Days 4 and 5—Extension Stage

Mr. Schiller starts the fourth day of the mineral unit with a review of the test results from Day 3. The class reexamines the data on their Mineral Identification Sheets, and each sample specimen is discussed. He leads a class conversation on what it means to be a "detective" and passes out the Sherlock Holmes book for students to begin reading as part of the literature connection to the science unit. Reading the Holmes book gets the students to bring in their "mineral detective" experiences into the language arts portion of curriculum. Mr. Schiller also announces that a geologist from a nearby college will be coming the next day to speak to the class about minerals and crystal types. During that presentation, students will construct models of crystal shapes to learn more about the different crystal forms found in their mineral specimens. The guest speaker will also relate crystal form to birthstones. And as a follow-up inquiry, each student will research which mineral (stone) is associated with the month of his or her birthday.

Day 6—Evaluation Stage

The unit concludes with a multidimensional assessment for content knowledge, identification skills, and inquiry attitudes. Mr. Schiller prepares a multiple-choice unit test on the concepts and vocabulary acquired during the investigations. As a hands-on component of the unit test, students are given an unknown mineral sample and asked to conduct

Specimen Name	Color	Other Properties	Hardness	Luster	Acid Test	Streak Test	Specimen Number
Calcite	cloudy white, other colors	3-way cleavage	3	glassy to dull	bubbles	white	
Galena	gray	very dense	2–3	metallic	no bubbles	gray	
Gypsum	white	splits in layers	2	dull	no bubbles	white	
Feldspar	white-brown	parallel layers	6	pearly	no bubbles	white	
Halite	clear	tastes salty	2–3	glassy	no bubbles	white	
Mica	clear or black	thin sheets	2–3	pearly	no bubbles	colorless	
Pyrite	goldlike	small cubic crystals	6–7	metallic	no bubbles	greenish black	
Quartz	clear or white	hexagon crystals	7	glassy	no bubbles	colorless	
Sulfur	yellow	soft and crumbles	1–2	greasy	no bubbles	yellowish white	
Talc	white	very soft	1	dull and pearly	no bubbles	white	

Figure 8.1 Mineral Identification Sheet

identification tests based on the format used during the previous days. As part of the language arts lesson that week, students are provided writing prompts to describe the skills detectives use in solving crime mysteries. The students are encouraged to write about their mineral detective experiences and relate it to the work scientists do in solving problems and finding the answers to questions they have. As students hand in their unit test, Mr. Schiller will remind the class to add other questions they have about minerals to the "Geology Bulletin Board" in the back of the room. These questions will spur further independent investigations.

STREAM TABLES—GRADES 9 THROUGH 12

JoAnn Moore is an exemplary earth science teacher in a large urban high school. In the beginning of the school year, tenth- and eleventh-grade students come to her class with scant experience in earth science from their elementary and middle school years. Nonetheless, despite the predominate number of students' initial aversion for the subject, over the course of the year, JoAnn will win them over to not only understanding geological topics but also appreciating the work geologists do and the impact that work has on everyday life.

Her "Water Cycle" unit is part of the statewide curriculum for high school earth science. To meet the state standards, JoAnn has devised a 10-week unit of study comprised of four sections: Bodies of Water (including oceans and lakes), Evapotranspiration (including cloud formation, precipitation, and weather), Stream Flow (including stream age, drainage patterns, erosion, and deposition), and Ground Water (including infiltration, porosity, and permeability). The following lessons describe a portion of JoAnn's section on Stream Flow. The lessons are based on the 5E Learning Cycle format and offer multiple activities and opportunities for student choice. JoAnn knows that capturing inner-city students' attention in earth science involves more than just the presentation of the subject matter. She has to capture their interest in geology as well.

The lesson format is divided into five sections: a demonstrated inquiry with a formative assessment that serves as the Engagement phase, a structured inquiry with choice options as part of the Exploration phase, a teacher-led presentation along with full-class discussion on drainage systems and erosion for the Explanation phase, a guided inquiry again with choice options for the Extension phase, and constructive response questions and performance tasks for the Evaluation phase.

Correlation: The overall objectives state that the students will determine the relationship among stream velocity, stream discharge, and slope. The Stream Tables lesson correlates to the National Science Education Standards (NRC, 1996) by stating that all students in Grades 9 through 12 should be able to do the following:

- Identify questions and concepts that guide scientific investigations (p. 175).
- Design and conduct scientific investigations (p. 175).

- Formulate and revise scientific explanations and models using logic and evidence (p. 175).
- Communicate and defend a scientific argument (p. 176).

The standards further state that students in Grades 9 through 12 should develop an understanding that "there are slow and progressive changes that result in problems for individuals and societies. For example, change in stream channel position, erosion of bridge foundations, sedimentation of lakes and harbors, coastal erosions, and continuing erosion of soil and landscapes can all negatively affect society" (NRC, 1996, p. 199).

Science Skills: Observing, measuring, hypothesizing, experimenting, collecting and displaying data, interpreting and analyzing data, forming models and explanations, and communicating

Materials:

- Stream tables with intake and outtake tubing
- Water supply
- Styrofoam "boats"
- Several one-inch blocks
- Graduated cylinders
- Sediment samples (fine sand, course sand, small pebbles, medium pebbles)
- Stopwatches (or wall clock with second hand)

Day-by-Day Lesson

On Day 1, the Engagement phase begins with a teacher-led demonstrated inquiry. JoAnn initiates the lesson by posing the question, "How does the gradient (angle) of a stream affect its flow (velocity)?" Before the demonstration begins, she writes the focus question on a sentence strip and tapes it to the board behind her. The question, being physically posted in the front of the room, helps students to concentrate on the purpose of the demonstration and reminds the teacher to return to the question as a review vehicle when closing the lesson. She also spends five minutes helping students clarify the purpose of the lesson to be sure they all understand the connection between the question and the demonstrated inquiry they are about to observe. Having completed that part, JoAnn is ready to proceed in demonstrating the effect of slope on stream flow. She calls on two students, Julie and John, to assist in the lesson.

JoAnn begins by positioning a stream table so the closed end is at the water supply (faucet) and the open end (or outtake) is at the sink. She then raises the closed end of the stream table by placing a one-inch block under the stream table. Julie is instructed to slowly turn in the faucet until a steady stream of water is flowing through the trough of the stream table. JoAnn places a Styrofoam boat at the top of the trough and releases the boat in the trough while John measures the time, in seconds, the boat takes to travel the entire length of the stream table. The other students record that time in their data tables.

JoAnn, Julie, and John repeat the procedure for a second and third trial. Again, the observing students record the data for Trials 2 and 3 in their data tables (see Figure 8.2).

Gradient	Trial 1 (in sec.)	Trial 2 (in sec.)	Trial 3 (in sec.)	Average (in sec.)	Velocity (cm/sec.)
Low					
Medium					
High					

Figure 8.2 Gradient and Stream Velocity

JoAnn now adds a second block to the end of the stream table, increasing the gradient by elevating the end to a height of two inches. Keeping the flow of water the same, the three demonstrators repeat the procedure for three trials as the other students record the results. Without hesitation, JoAnn places a third block to the end of the stream table elevating the end to a height of three inches. Again, they repeat the procedure for three trials as the observers record the results in the appropriate column of the data table.

JoAnn now instructs the students to calculate the average stream velocity for all three gradients using the following formula:

$$\text{Stream velocity} = \frac{\text{Length of trough (cm)}}{\text{Average time (in seconds)}}$$

At the end of the demonstration, JoAnn has students draw an appropriate graph to show the relationship between stream gradient (angle) and its velocity. She returns to the focus question posted on the board at the beginning of the lesson and uses that to initiate a class discussion on the relationship between the two variables. JoAnn wraps up the lesson by encouraging the class to make some assumptions about the effect of slope on stream flow.

Following the discussion, JoAnn hands out a brief formative assessment sheet (Figure 8.3) where students calculate stream velocity for various slopes.

Demonstrating What You Know

Using a faucet, a two-meter trough, a ping-pong ball, a stopwatch, and a protractor, Jennifer and Jessica want to investigate how the slope of the trough affects the velocity of flowing water. They elevate one end of the trough to form four different angles: 5, 10, 15, and 20 degrees. Using a medium flow of water from the faucet, Jennifer places a ping-pong ball at the top of the trough and releases it. Jessica times how long it takes the ball to reach the bottom of the trough. The table below shows their results.

Angle of trough (degrees)	Length of trough (meters)	Time (seconds)	Velocity (meters/second)
5	2	6.6	
10	2	5.6	
15	2	4.9	
20	2	4.2	

Figure 8.3 Jennifer and Jessica's Water Flow Data

Use the data to calculate the velocity of the water for each angle and form an explanation describing the relationship between angle and velocity.

On Days 2 and 3, the Exploration phase, students choose one of three structured inquiries that build upon the demonstrated inquiry from the previous day. The choices are as follows:

1. How does stream discharge affect the stream velocity?

2. How does the gradient or angle of the trough affect the sediment wash?

3. How does stream discharge affect the sediment wash?

JoAnn begins the next phase of the Stream Tables unit by posting the three questions on the board and explaining to the class that, as individuals, they will choose a question to explore, follow the directions on the structured inquiry provided, collect and analyze data, and report their findings to the class. She gives them several minutes to read over the questions once again and decide which question best suits their interest. The students then convene in groups of three to start their investigations. Various supplies and materials are available in the front of the room, although JoAnn has purposely not listed the materials needed for each of the three investigations. Some of the equipment and supplies are needed; others act as distracters to build students' decision-making skills. She feels that enhancing student decision making is one of the goals of inquiry-based learning. Although there seems to be some confusion at first, students gradually settle into deciding what they will need to complete the investigations. As she watches the groups become absorbed in their assignments, JoAnn thinks to herself, "It's all part of the learning process."

Each of the three structured inquiries are provided as follows:

Question 1: How does stream discharge (stream load) affect the stream velocity (as measured by the speed of a Styrofoam "boat")?

Procedure:

1. Position a stream table so the closed end is at the water supply (faucet) and the open end (or outtake) is at the sink.

2. Raise the closed end of the stream table by placing one one-inch block under the stream table.

3. Slowly turn in the faucet until you have a relatively low flow stream of water flowing through the trough of the stream table.

4. Place a Styrofoam boat at the top of the trough. As you release the boat in the trough, measure the time in seconds the boat takes to travel the entire length of the stream table.

5. Design a data table to record your results. (See sample Figure 8.4.)

(Continued)

(Continued)

Stream Discharge	Trial 1 (in sec.)	Trial 2 (in sec.)	Trial 3 (in sec.)	Average (in sec.)	Velocity (cm/sec.)
Low					
Medium					
High					

Figure 8.4   Discharge and Stream Velocity

6. Record that time in your data table.

7. Repeat Steps 4 and 5 for a second and third trial. Record the data for Trials 2 and 3 in your data table.

8. Readjust the faucet to a medium flow rate.

9. Repeat Steps 4 and 5 for three trials and place the results in the data table.

10. Readjust the faucet to a high flow rate.

11. Repeat the procedure for three trials and record the results in the data table.

12. Draw an appropriate graph to show the relationship between stream flow and velocity.

13. Based on the data collected, form a concluding statement from your investigation.

Question 2: How does the gradient or angle of the trough affect the sediment wash?

Procedure:

1. Position a stream table so the closed end is at the water supply (faucet) and the open end (or outtake) is at the sink.

2. Raise the closed end of the stream table by placing one one-inch block under the stream table.

3. Slowly turn in the faucet until you have a steady stream of water flowing through the trough of the stream table.

4. Using a graduated cylinder, measure 10 milliliters of fine sand.

5. Pour the sand in the top (raised end) of the trough.

6. Measure the time (in seconds) the sand takes to travel the entire length of the stream table and the trough is completely clean of sand particles.

7. Design a data table to record and organize your results.

8. Record that time in your data table. (See sample Figure 8.5.)

Gradient	Volume of Sand (mL)	Trial 1 (in sec.)	Trial 2 (in sec.)	Trial 3 (in sec.)	Average (in sec.)	Stream Load (mL/sec.)
Low						
Medium						
High						

Figure 8.5   Gradient and Stream Load

9. Repeat Steps 4 and 5 for a second and third trial. Record your data for Trials 2 and 3 in your data table.

10. Add a second block to the end of the stream table elevating the end to a height of two inches.

11. Keeping the flow of water the same, repeat Steps 4 and 5 for three trials and place your results in the data table.

12. Add a third block to the end of the stream table elevating the end to a height of three inches. Repeat the procedure for three trials and record your results in the data table.

13. Calculate the average stream velocity for all three heights using the following formula:

$$\text{Stream wash} = \frac{\text{Milliliters of sand (10 mL)}}{\text{Average time (in seconds)}}$$

14. Draw an appropriate graph to show the relationship between stream gradient (angle) and sediment wash.

15. Based on the data collected, form a concluding statement from your investigation.

Question 3: How does stream discharge (stream load) affect the sediment wash?

Procedure:

1. Position a stream table so the closed end is at the water supply (faucet) and the open end (or outtake) is at the sink.

2. Raise the closed end of the stream table by placing two one-inch blocks under the stream table.

3. Slowly turn in the faucet until you have a low stream of water flowing through the trough of the stream table.

4. Using a graduated cylinder, measure 10 milliliters of fine sand.

(Continued)

(Continued)

5. Pour the sand in the top (raised end) of the trough.

6. Measure the time (in seconds) the sand takes to travel the entire length of the stream table and the trough is completely clean of sand particles.

7. Design a data table to record and organize your results.

8. Record that time in your data table. (See sample Figure 8.6.)

Stream Discharge	Volume of Sand (mL)	Trial 1 (in sec.)	Trial 2 (in sec.)	Trial 3 (in sec.)	Average (in sec.)	Stream Load (mL/sec.)
Low						
Medium						
High						

Figure 8.6 Discharge and Stream Load

9. Repeat Steps 4 and 5 for a second and third trial. Record your data for Trials 2 and 3 in your data table.

10. Adjust the flow of water to a medium flow, repeat Steps 4 and 5 for three trials, and place your results in the data table.

11. Adjust the flow of water to a high rate. Repeat the procedure for three trials and record your results in the data table.

12. Calculate the average stream velocity for all three heights using the following formula:

$$\text{Stream load} = \frac{\text{Milliliters of sand (10 mL)}}{\text{Average time (in seconds)}}$$

13. Draw an appropriate graph to show the relationship between stream discharge (load) and sediment wash.

14. Based on the data collected, form a concluding statement from your investigation.

During Day 4, the Explanation phase, JoAnn starts the lesson by having each group communicate the findings of its inquiry to the rest of the class. She gives time for the groups to share their newly acquired knowledge and then, through a teacher-led discussion and lecture, introduces the concept of drainage systems and erosion.

She explains to the students that water flows downhill by the pull of gravity to the lowest spot in the area. As the water flows to the low spots, it carves out a channel in the land and moves rock sediment and particles. The more water, the more erosion and channeling take place. She explains that the channels in which the water flows are called streams. Small streams then join together, forming a drainage system (basin) for the area. The streams eventually drain into a river, lake, or larger body of water.

This presentation leads to knowing how a drainage divide determines a drainage pattern in an area. She further questions students concerning how the type of bedrock influences the drainage system in an area and how the quality and type of topsoil influence the particle flow of the stream. Using topographic maps, students then study the drainage systems for their local areas as well as statewide systems, and later, using colored pencils, trace drainage basins for their state and shade areas to identify the watershed for their local areas.

Days 5 and 6, the Extension phase, involve two guided inquiries. Again, choice is a significant aspect of the lesson. In this phase, students choose any one task to investigate by designing and carrying out a procedure. At the end of the Extension phase, students should be able to do the following:

1. Predict the relationship between stream load and angle to particle wash.

2. Design an investigation to test their prediction.

3. State and describe the relationship between the two variables.

4. Explain rate of erosion based on the two variables.

Since this part of the Stream Tables unit is similar to the process from the Exploration phase, students are becoming accustomed to the culture of Ms. Moore's classroom where they are expected to make decisions for their own learning. As one of her best students comments, "Ms. Moore is here to guide us. We are the ones who need to take responsibility and channel our energies into our own learning."

The two choice options are as follows:

Task 1: Design and carry out an investigation that will determine how stream flow affects particle size wash. (Hint: Consider using various-size sediment particles available at the supply table to answer your question.)

Task 2: Design and carry out an investigation that will determine how the angle of the trough affects particle size wash. (Hint: Consider using various-size sediment particles available at the supply table to answer your question.)

Knowing that students' interests and abilities vary within each class, JoAnn often offers a third option: a self-directed investigation. In this option, students can draw from their investigations during the Engagement and Exploration phases to design their own self-directed question to investigate.

On Day 7, The Evaluation phase involves both constructed response questions and performance tasks. Several constructed response questions follow:

1. What two factors have the greatest effect on stream flow (velocity)?

2. What is the relationship between stream gradient and stream velocity?

3. A cork boat travels the length of a 100 cm stream table in 15 seconds. Calculate the rate of change (velocity) of the cork boat.

4. From their initial investigation about stream slope and stream velocity, Jennifer and Jessica thought of another question to investigate. They wanted to find out how particle size affects the rate of erosion. They used a faucet, a two-meter trough, a stopwatch, and various-size particles. They elevated one end of the trough to form an angle of 10 degrees. Using a medium flow of water from the faucet, Jennifer poured 50 milliliters of fine sand at the top of the trough. As she turned on the faucet to a medium flow, Jessica timed how long it took for the particles to completely wash to the bottom of the trough. The table that follows (Figure 8.7) shows their results.

Sediment Particles	Angle of Trough (Degrees)	Amount of Particles (Milliliters)	Length of Trough (Meters)	Time (Seconds)
Fine sand (.005 cm)	10	50	2	14.6
Coarse sand (.010 cm)	10	50	2	25.6
Small pebbles (.25 cm)	10	50	2	44.9
Large pebbles (.50 cm)	10	50	2	74.2

Figure 8.7 Jennifer and Jessica's Water Flow Data

Use the data to summarize the results and describe the relationship between particle size and the rate of erosion. Explain how variation in particle shape can affect the rate of erosion rate.

For the Evaluation phase, JoAnn provides two authentic performance tasks from which students can choose one. For the tasks, students again form groups of three to complete the project. The two options are as follows:

Choice 1—Researching Erosion

Choose one agent of erosion (gravity, wind, running water, waves, or human influence) as a topic for a research project. Using books, websites, and articles, identify and describe a local area of erosion. Include pictures of the source of erosion and damage caused by the eroding factor. Display your findings to the class on a tri-fold poster, PowerPoint slide presentation, or written report.

Choice 2—Report to a Governmental Committee

Choose one agent of erosion (gravity, wind, running water, waves, or human influence) that affects your neighborhood, town, village, or local community. Prepare an oral report to a governmental committee regarding the cause and source of erosion. Provide diagrams of the area along with one proposal for the committee to consider rectifying the situation. Make an oral presentation to the class as a rehearsal to your presentation to the governmental committee.

With the earth science investigation we just read, Rob Schiller and JoAnn Moore provide two examples of differentiated units of study with opportunities for choice. Equally challenging, balancing several investigations going on simultaneously in a classroom or lab takes quite a bit of instructional juggling. JoAnn humorously describes her role as a teacher like a circus juggler. "Differentiated teaching," she says, "is a lot like juggling balls in the air. Juggling requires concentration of your surroundings and the ability to react. I do that every day in my science classes."

WRITING QUESTIONS FOR REFLECTION AND DISCUSSION

As you did in the proceeding chapters, from the readings in Chapter 8, write three questions that concern you. Share and discuss your questions and responses with a colleague.

1.

2.

3.

Differentiated Physical Science Inquiries

In this chapter, you will find two examples of differentiated physical science inquiries being applied to elementary and middle school classrooms.

INVESTIGATING M&M'S— GRADES 3 THROUGH 5

Introduction: Johnnie Wong is a third- and fourth-grade "looping" teacher at Elmwood Elementary School. Looping is an instructional practice in which a class of children stays with a teacher for two or more grade levels. At Elmwood, the children and teacher remain together for just two years. At the end of the second year, the children move on to a new teacher while Mr. Wong returns to third grade for a new group of students.

The benefits of looping are twofold. The overwhelming research indicates that students, since they are already familiar with the teacher, display less anxiety and uneasiness at the start of the second school year cycle. Looping also promotes continuity and more personal relationships between the teacher and the students. For teachers like Mr. Wong, the benefits of looping consist of becoming more familiar with the intellectual, emotional, and social development of each child in his class. Working with students for two years helps Mr. Wong to better understand their particular learning styles, needs, and individual personalities—a prerequisite for differentiated instruction. Working with children for a second year also helps him to build a sense of community and a healthy relationship with parents and caregivers as well. Furthermore, the two-year cycle reduces time spent on "getting to know" each other. Mr. Wong need not start from scratch at the beginning of the school year, learning new sets of names and personalities and establishing classroom rules and expectations. Since looping facilitates a more efficient classroom, Mr. Wong estimates that looping reaps a month of instructional time at the beginning of the second year. As he often says, "Looping avoids a lot of the shenanigans that go along with having to start a new school year off on the right foot."

Johnnie Wong just started his second year with his present fourth graders. Although Johnnie enjoys teaching science and integrates science into all of the other academic subjects, the students' prior teacher (looping in Grades 1 and 2) provided little science instruction. Her major emphasis was in developing reading and writing skills. When the students arrive in Mr. Wong's class as third graders, to them, science is a new and exciting subject. During their first year together as third graders, Johnnie introduces the children to hands-on science. At first, since this is a relatively new experience, there is much for the students to learn about working and thinking like fledgling scientists. For the first year of the looping cycle, Johnnie emphasizes prescribed science activities from the district's science textbook program where the procedures and steps of the "experiment" are clearly laid out. However, during the second year, Johnnie is now ready to have the children move on to designing their own investigations and making their own predictions about the outcome of those investigations. In this series of lessons, Mr. Wong will use M&M candies to provide students with an opportunity to learn the skill of predicting. In follow-up activities, students will distinguish between a prediction and a hypothesis and design investigations to test their hypotheses.

Estimated Time of Lesson: Three to four days

Correlation: Investigating M&M's aligns to the National Science Education Standards (NRC, 1996) for Grades K–4:

- Ask a question about objects, organisms, and event in the environment (p. 122).
- Plan and conduct a simple investigation (p. 122).
- Use data to construct a reasonable explanation (p. 122).
- Communicate investigations and explanations (p. 122).
- Objects have many observable properties, including size, weight, shape, color, temperature, and the ability to react with other substances (p. 126).

Science Skills: Observing, predicting, forming hypotheses, designing experiments, controlling variables, organizing and analyzing data, making generalizations, communicating

Background Information:

In 1976, red dye 2 was thought to be a cancer-causing agent. Although red M&M's did not contain any red dye 2, the color was removed from the M&M package due to consumer fears. Ten years later in March 1987, the red color returned using red dye 3 and 40, as before. Blue M&M's were added in 1997.

Materials:

- One king-size (3.18 oz.) bag of M&M's
- One package containing approximately 25 small bags of M&M's for each student
- One "Predicting and Graphing With M&M's" sheet for each student
- One clear plastic petri dish (or small Styrofoam plate) for each student
- One package of Skittles
- One package of Gobstoppers
- Room-temperature water
- Science journals

Prior Setup: King-size bags of M&M's are usually available in grocery and candy stores. The package of 25 small bags, however, may be more difficult to find. They are always available during Halloween. As a safety issue, eating candy in class can be a concern for some teachers. Although the children may be tempted to eat the M&M's they experiment with, you may want to provide "clean" M&M's for eating.

Day-by-Day Lessons

Day 1: Predicting and Graphing With M&M's—a Structured Inquiry

On Day 1, Mr. Wong introduces the lesson by asking students, "Guess how old I am." With responses anywhere between 25 and 37, Johnnie helps the students to understand what it means to make a guess. He explains, "When you make a guess, you give your opinion about something with limited or uncertain information or evidence." Next, Johnnie holds up a large glass jar full of M&M's and asks, "How many M&M's would you guess are in the jar?" As the children respond, he places several of their answers on the board and points out the range of guesses from the students' responses. He moves on to ask, "What information would you need to make an accurate guess?" One of the children replies that she would need to count the number of M&M's on the top layer and then multiply that number by the possible number of layers of M&M's in the jar. Mr. Wong goes on to explain that when you make a guess, you have little or no, or even biased, information to answer the question. But when you make a prediction, you use information and evidence to project or foretell an outcome of a result or an event. Next, he invites the students to recall when they were asked to make a guess and when they were asked to make a prediction. "Now, let's see; how we can use M&M candies to help us learn to make good predictions?" Mr. Wong adds.

Holding up the large bag of M&M's, Mr. Wong presents the following task to the class: Predict the number of each color of M&M's in this king-size bag. "But before we do that," he states, "let's first use whatever prior information you have to make a guess as to the number of red, orange, yellow, green, blue, and brown M&M's in this large bag. Your total number of M&M's should equal 100 pieces. You can record that guess in the first column of your data worksheet titled, 'My Guess of Large Bag'" (Figure 9.1).

M&M's Data Table

Color Code	My Guess of Large Bag	My Results of Small Bag	My Prediction of Large Bag	Class Prediction of Large Bag	Actual Amount of Large Bag
Rd = red					
Or = orange					
Yl = yellow					
Gr = green					
Bl = blue					
Br = brown					
Total	100		100	100	

Figure 9.1

Mr. Wong then begins to clarify that more information is needed in order to predict the number of each color in the large bag. Distributing a small bag of M&M's to each child, the children open their bags and graph the small bag of M&M's (approximately 25) by placing one candy piece in the appropriate square on the blank graph (Figures 9.2 and 9.3) and recording the distribution of colors for their small bag in the "My Results of Small Bag" column.

The results trigger a discussion as to which color of M&M has the largest number. The class finally agrees that there are more browns than any other color.

Michael, one of the top students in the class, proposes that they use the results from the small bag to make a prediction for the large bag. Mr. Wong acknowledges Michael's proposal and asks if there are any other suggestions from the class. The class unanimously likes Michael's idea. Using the data from the small bag (containing about 25 M&M's), Mr. Wong has them record their predictions for the king-size bag (containing about 100 M&M's) in the "My Prediction of Large Bag" column.

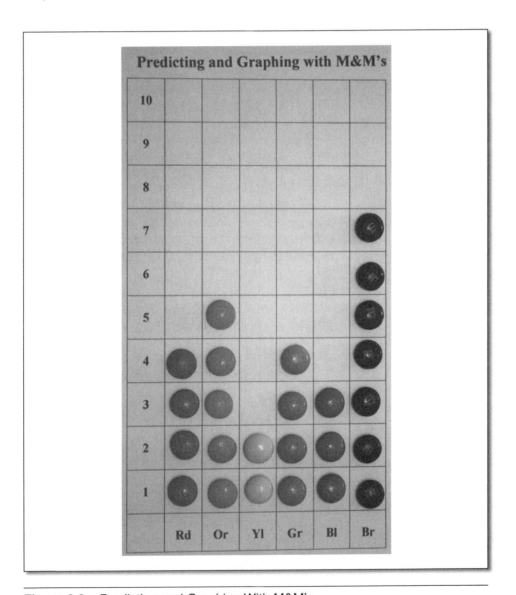

Figure 9.2   Predicting and Graphing With M&M's

Predicting and Graphing With M&M's

	Rd	Or	Yl	Gr	Bl	Br
10						
9						
8						
7						
6						
5						
4						
3						
2						
1						

Color code: Rd = red, Or = orange, Yl = yellow, Gr = green, Bl = blue, Br = brown

Figure 9.3

Prompting the students to consider making a full-class prediction, Johnnie asks, "How could we use the most amount of data available to make our prediction even better?" At this point, Tianna suggests making a class prediction using the data from all the individual small bags. Anticipating this answer, Mr. Wong produces a large data chart (Figure 9.4) where each student can record his or her individual results of the small bag to determine the class average and thus a class prediction.

After each student records his or her small bag results on the large data chart, two students volunteer to calculate the average for each color. Mr. Wong leads the class into making a full-class prediction for the large bag. After the class prediction is made and recorded under the "Class Prediction of Large Bag" column, it is now time to open the king-size bag, count the actual number of different colors of M&M's in the bag, and determine which was more accurate—individual guesses, the individual predictions, or the class prediction.

As the students analyze their data, Mr. Wong points out the variation in the class results. Several students are asked to draw conclusions from the evidence and form explanations as to why the class prediction was closer to the actual amount of the large bag versus the guesses and the individual predictions. At the end of the day's lesson, the students summarize that the more data you have, the more accurate your prediction will probably be.

Day 2: M&M's in Water—a Guided Inquiry

At the start of the science lesson for Day 2, the students review their predictions and findings from the previous day. "Today," Mr. Wong begins, "we will make some observations and predictions about the properties of M&M's." As he passes out several M&M's to each student, they are asked to observe the candy's shape, size, and color, as well as its properties both inside and out. The students are told to record those observations in their science journals.

Mr. Wong recalls that when he was young, the voice from the M&M's commercial said, "M&M's melt in your mouth, not in your hands." Using that as a springboard for inquiry, he poses the question, "What would happen if you placed an M&M in a container of water? What do you predict would happen?" His question sparks an activity where students are given half a petri dish (either the top or bottom half) half filled with room-temperature water. But before the students place the M&M in the water, they have to make a prediction and record it in their journal.

After the students are told to place the M&M's in the water with the "M" side facing up, the students begin to notice that the M&M coating begins to dissolve, forming circular-like rings around the candy. (See Figure 9.5.) Several students shout with excitement that the colored coating is dissolving into the water. "I'm melting; I'm melting," one student exclaims. Michael notices that the color seems to settle to the bottom of the dish while the letter M seems to separate from the candy coating and float to the top. Much to her surprise, Ali observes that there is an inner white layer just beneath the outer colored layer! The investigation sparks a lot of new discoveries for the children.

Number of M&M Colors in Each Small Bag

Student Bag	1	2	3	4	5	6	7	8	9	10	Total	Average	Percentage
Red													
Orange													
Yellow													
Green													
Blue													
Brown													

Figure 9.4

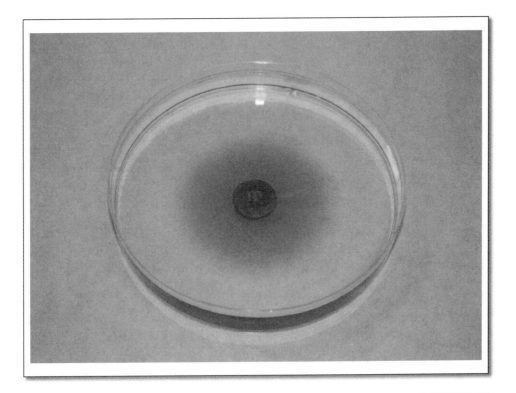

Figure 9.5

Mr. Wong uses the excitement to suggest that students now think of questions they would like to investigate about the properties of M&M's. He says that their next inquiries will involve making a special kind of prediction—a hypothesis—and explains the meaning of the scientific term. As the lesson closes, the children are asked to choose a question to investigate, form small groups from those choosing the same question, and design a procedure to answer the question. And for the first time, these young scientists will write a hypothesis to test.

Days 3 and 4: More Investigations About M&M's

On Day 3, students bring in any special supplies and materials they need to conduct their investigations. Some students choose to work alone, while others choose to work in groups of two. The questions the class generates include the following:

- Do all colors of M&M's dissolve at the same rate?
- Do plain M&M's dissolve at the same rate as peanut M&M's?
- Will the coating on the M&M dissolve any faster in warm water than in cold water?
- What would happen if we place two or three different colors next to each other in the same petri dish filled with water?
- Do M&M's dissolve faster in tap water, distilled water, carbonated water, or bottled water?
- How does adding sugar or salt to the water affect the dissolving rate?
- Do M&M's dissolve in other liquids (such as Sprite, Coke, milk, or lemonade) like they do in water?

- Do other candies, like Skittles or Gobstoppers, dissolve the same way the M&M's do?
- Does stirring the water increase the dissolving rate of M&M's?
- How can you make an M&M dissolve the fastest? The slowest?

For their self-directed inquiries, each individual or group of students writes their question on a sentence strip and posts it at their work area. This way, Mr. Wong can easily identify what question each child or group is working on. He reminds students to collect evidence to support or refute their hypothesis. At the end of the lesson, students begin to organize their results in preparation for the next day, when they explain their conclusions to the rest of the class. The students have a choice in how they will present their observations and findings as recorded in their journals—either as an oral report, as a single-sided poster board or tri-fold board, as a PowerPoint presentation, or as a one-page written lab report.

On Day 4, the final day, each student or small group gives a three-minute presentation that outlines their hypothesis, their supporting evidence, and an explanation of the new information they discovered. The audience is encouraged to politely raise questions and challenge the presenter's claims and evidence with counterclaims. Mr. Wong emphasizes that good scientists challenge ideas, not the person presenting the idea. At the end of the M&M inquiry, students make their first step into understanding the meaning of a scientific investigation and argumentation. In follow-up inquiries later in the school year, Mr. Wong will emphasize the purpose of identifying and controlling variables in an investigation, as well as more involved methods of data collection and organization.

Other Resources:

Jorgenson, O., Cleveland, J., & Vanosdall, R. (2004). *Doing good science in middle school: A practical guide to inquiry-based instruction* (Chapter 6, Activity 8—"Gobstoppers"). Arlington, VA: NSTA Press.

Kessler, J., & Galvan, P. (2005). *Inquiry in action: Investigating matter through inquiry.* Washington, DC: American Chemical Society. Now available online at http://www.inquiryinaction.org/

M&M's web page—http://www.mms.com/us/

Wafler, E. (2001). Inspired inquiry: Using candy and containers of water to spark students' interest in investigating. *Science and Children, 38*(4), 28–31.

DROPPER POPPERS—GRADES 6 THROUGH 8

Introduction: In this activity, seventh-grade students in Mrs. Gardner's class will investigate the principles of energy transformation. The Dropper Poppers (see Figure 9.6) activity is also suitable for introducing the concepts of potential and kinetic energy. Although this activity is intended for children in Grades 6 through 8, it can adapted for other grades as well. Andrea Del Zappa from Aitken High School in Aitken, Minnesota, adapts the lesson to her high school physics class (see: "Launching a Ping Pong Ball With a Dropper Popper" at http://serc.carleton .edu/sp/mnstep/activities/27442.html).

Estimated Time of Lesson: One to two class periods

Correlation: The objective of the lesson is to explore the concept of energy and motion and determine how the release point of bouncing objects affects its rebound. Dropper Poppers aligns to the National Science Education Standards (NRC, 1996) for Grades 5 through 8:

- Design and conduct a scientific investigation (p. 145).
- Develop descriptions, explanations, predictions, and models using explanations (p. 145).
- Think critically and logically to make the relationship between evidence and explanations (p. 145).
- The motion of an object can be described by its position, direction, and speed (p. 154).

Misconceptions: Because of their prior experiences with bouncing balls, students may have the notion that the higher the rubber ball is dropped, the higher it will bounce. Similarly, applying that same observation and principle to the Poppers, students may also think that the higher the Popper is released, the higher it will bounce or rebound. This is where the Dropper Poppers provide a discrepant event that runs counterintuitively to children's normal experiences. It's also when the fun begins!

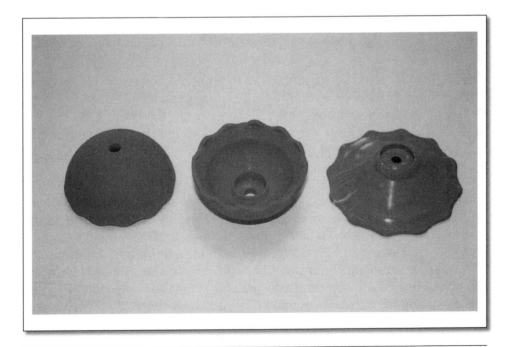

Figure 9.6 Photo of Dropper Popper

Background Information: According to the NRC (1996), "The study of motion and the forces causing motion provide concrete experiences on which a more comprehensive understanding of force can be based in Grades 9 through 12. By using simple objects, . . . students can move from qualitative to quantitative descriptions of moving objects and begin to describe the forces acting on the objects" (p. 154).

In the Dropper Popper stations, students will investigate whether or not the height of the release point affects the distance the Popper will bounce (rebound). Contrary to most students' predictions, the amount of energy in the Poppers is determined more by the potential energy stored in the inverted Popper and resiliency of the Popper than by the height of the release point.

When the Popper hits the floor, its potential energy is converted to kinetic energy (the rebound of the Popper). The height at which the Popper is dropped acts as a catalyst for reverting the Popper back into its original form. Thus, all the Poppers, regardless of the height dropped, will rebound to approximately the same height with some minor variability. But note—dropping a Popper at a low height may not provide enough energy to revert the Popper to its original shape. In addition, a slight amount of energy is "absorbed" if the Popper is dropped on a carpeted surface versus a wooden or tiled surface.

Materials:

- Several Dropper Poppers—available from Arbor Scientific (arborsci .com), Educational Innovations (teacherscource.com), or Steve Spangler Science (stevespanglerscience.com)
- Assorted rubber balls and super balls
- "Happy and Unhappy Balls" (optional)—also available from Arbor Scientific
- Measuring tapes
- 12" × 12" pieces of carpet and tile flooring
- Science journals

Prior Setup: To avoid congestion, Station A should be set up in a separate room. Materials for each station should be readily available in a clear plastic baggie or cardboard box. Describe to the class the procedure and the level of structure for each station. Emphasize that students have a choice in selecting the station that best fits their preferred learning style, interest, and need for structure.

The Setting: Mrs. Gardner's seventh graders at Millburn Middle School are studying energy transfer in their physical science course. Earlier in the energy unit, students brought in household toys to show how mechanical and electrical energy is transferred to motion, sound, and light energy. Now they are moving on to potential and kinetic energy transfer. In the Dropper Popper activity, students will now test how the height of the release point of a bouncing object affects how high that object will rebound. To do this, they will utilize several science process skills such as observing, measuring, experimenting, collecting and analyzing data, formulating explanations, and communicating.

The Four Stations

Since Mrs. Gardner decided to have a demonstrated inquiry for this lesson, she recruits the help of a parent volunteer, Dr. Seager, who is also a mechanical engineer at a manufacturing plant in the community. Dr. Seager will be the additional adult required for Station A. Station A is set up in another room across the hall. Mrs. Gardner introduces the lesson and the four choices students have for this energy transfer lesson.

Station A: As a Demonstrated Inquiry

For the students who choose the demonstrated inquiry, Dr. Seager starts Station A with a quick demonstration. He holds a super ball above the demonstration table at a height of two feet and asks the students, "What will happen when I drop the ball?" One student responds that it will bounce back up. "Good," says Dr. Seager, "that's what called a prediction. Now, let's test that prediction." He then drops the super ball and affirms the prediction that the ball did indeed bounce back up as expected. "If I now hold the super ball up to a height of three feet, what will happen to the height of the rebound? Will the ball bounce higher or lower?"

Students shout out a resounding reply, "Higher."

"Well, then, let's test that prediction too," says Dr. Seager as he once again drops the ball and affirms the students' second prediction. He then shows the students a Dropper Popper and asks them to make a prediction for the Popper as they did for the super ball. He proceeds to write the focus question on the board: How does the height at which the Popper is released affect the height the Popper rebounds? Using the observation from the super ball, the students unanimously agree that the higher the Popper is released, the higher it will rebound.

Dr. Seager pushes the outer curve of the Popper inward and holds it over the tabletop. He asks for a student volunteer to hold a measuring tape to measure the distance of the rebound. Moving the Popper to a height of 12 inches, he releases it by dropping the flat side down and announces the height of the rebound. He then instructs the students to construct a data table to record and organize the results. He leads them to design a data table similar to Figure 9.7.

Dr. Seager repeats the same procedure for Trials 2 and 3 while the students record the results from all three trials in their data table. He repeats the procedure for 24, 36, 48, and 50 inches. For each height, the students record the results in their data table and calculate the average.

Using the data collected, the students determine that their prediction was different from what they expected. One student asked, "The data show that the height the Popper was dropped did not affect how far it bounced. Why is that?" Dr. Seager goes on to explain that potential energy is "stored" in the inverted Popper and is converted to kinetic energy when the Popper hits the surface of the table and snaps back to its original shape. "The potential energy in the Popper determines how high it rebounds, not the height at which it's dropped," he says.

Dr. Seager then describes the work that scientists and engineers do. He explains that sometimes what is predicted to happen may not always happen. "That's what makes the jobs scientists and engineers do so

	Distance the Popper Rebounded (In Inches)			
	Trial 1	**Trial 2**	**Trial 3**	**Average**
12"				
24"				
36"				
48"				
50"				

Figure 9.7   Dropper Popper Data Table

interesting." To whet the students' appetites for another discrepancy, Dr. Seager brings out two small identical-looking black balls (see "Happy and Unhappy Balls" in materials list). He asks the students if the balls are the same, and while holding them, one in each hand at the same height above the tabletop, he asks what will happen to the balls when he releases them. Most of the students predict that the balls will bounce back up. When he drops the balls simultaneously, one ball bounces back up while the other drops flat to the tabletop with no bounce at all. "Wow," exclaims a student, "what's going on?"

Dr. Seager leaves the students in a state of wonder and amazement saying, "That, my fellow scientists, will be answered tomorrow by Mrs. Gardner!"

Station B: As a Structured Inquiry

At Station B, students are provided a worksheet with a question to be investigated and a list of procedures to follow. When they arrive at Station B, students will choose a partner and begin the investigation without further prompting. The following shows the handout for Station B:

Question: How does the height at which the Popper is released affect the height the Popper rebounds?

Prediction: Write a prediction in your science journal to answer the question.

Materials:

- One Dropper Popper
- One measuring tape
- One roll of masking tape (optional)

Procedure:

1. Push the outer curve of the Popper inward.

2. Place the Popper over a hard floor surface at a height of 12 inches.

3. Release the Popper by dropping it flat side down.

4. Using the measuring tape, measure the distance (in inches) the Popper rebounds.

5. In your science journal, design a data table to record and organize your results. (Note: If students have difficulty designing their own data table, the teacher may choose to provide one. See Resource F.)

6. Repeat the same procedure for Trials 2 and 3. Record the results from all three trials in the data table.

7. Repeat the same procedure for 24, 36, 48, and 50 inches. Record the results in the data table.

8. Calculate the average for each height. Show your work.

Conclusion: Using the data collected, decide if the prediction you made earlier was correct or not. Form an explanation that is supported by the evidence.

Station C: As a Guided Inquiry

At Station C, students are provided a worksheet with an opening exploration to spark interest in the tasks. When they arrive at Station C, students will choose a partner to work with and begin the investigation with further prompting. The following shows the handout for Station C:

Carry out the opening exploration and then choose one or more of the tasks below to complete.

Procedure for Opening Exploration:

1. Push the outer curve of the Popper inward.
2. Place the Popper over a hard floor surface at a height of 12 inches.
3. Release the Popper by dropping it flat side down.
4. Using the measuring tape, measure the distance (in inches) the Popper rebounds.

Tasks to Complete:

- Task 1: Design and carry out an investigation to determine how the height a Popper is released affects the height it will rebound. Draw an illustration of the design and record all your data in your science journal.
- Task 2: Design and carry out an investigation to determine how the height a rubber ball or super ball is released affects the height it will rebound. Draw an illustration of the design and record all your data in your science journal. Compare the results of the Popper to the rubber and super balls.
- Task 3: Design and carry out an investigation to determine how the surface a Popper is dropped on affects the height it will rebound. Draw an illustration of the design and record all your data in your science journal.
- Task 4: Design and carry out an investigation to have the Popper rebound to a height of just 48 inches. Draw an illustration of the design and record all your data in your science journal.

At the completion of the task(s), write a summary explanation from the data collected. Be prepared to share your findings and explanations with the rest of the class. Choose a means to share your results (oral presentation, PowerPoint, poster, or written report). Consider other follow-up investigations that you could conduct as a result of your initial findings.

Station D: As a Self-Directed Inquiry

Like Station C, at Station D students are provided a worksheet with an opening exploration to spark interest in designing a follow-up experiment. When they arrive at Station D, students will choose a partner and begin the investigation without further prompting. The following shows the handout for Station D:

Carry out the opening exploration and then choose one or more of the tasks below to complete.

Procedure for Opening Exploration:

1. Push the outer curve of the Popper inward.

2. Place the Popper over a hard floor surface at a height of 12 inches.

3. Release the Popper by dropping it flat side down.

4. Using the measuring tape, measure the distance (in inches) the Popper rebounds.

Follow-Up Task:

Using the materials at the station, investigate the different factors or variables that affect the height a Popper will rebound. In your science journal, write a specific claim for each investigation and collect and record the evidence to support or refute the claim made. Be prepared to share your findings and explanations to the rest of the class. Choose a means to share your results (oral presentation, PowerPoint, poster, or written report). Consider follow-up investigations that you could conduct as a result of your initial findings. Your teacher has various balls and objects available to stimulate other investigations to think about.

Investigating M&M's and the Dropper Popper activities offer various avenues to differentiate science investigations as described in Chapter 3 and to engage your students in opportunities for choice. For a demonstration of the Dropper Popper, called "Dopper Popper Energy Transformation" by Arbor Scientific, see TeacherTube.com. See also http://www.teachertube.com/viewVideo.php?video_id=55094&title=Dopper_Popper_Energy_Transformation. (Note: The TeacherTube website indicates "Dopper Popper," not "Dropper Popper.")

WRITING QUESTIONS FOR
REFLECTION AND DISCUSSION

As you did in previous chapters, from the readings in Chapter 9, write three questions that concern you. Again, your questions, the self-directed questions, are the most meaningful in understanding the DSI approach. Share and discuss your questions and responses with a colleague and keep the lines of communication open between you and others interested in differentiating your science inquiry lessons.

1.

2.

3.

Making a Commitment to Differentiated Science Inquiry

AN ANIMAL STORY—THE EPILOGUE

Do you remember the animal school tale from the Preface? Well, there's an ending to the story. It seems, at the close of the school's first year, the animal elders were puzzled by the results of the school's Annual Performance Review (APR). The report highlighted an alarming dropout rate of groundhogs and indicated less-than-stellar performance from the other animals for all the school's courses. "How could this be?" asked one elder. "We offer the courses needed to successfully compete in our woodland community."

"Yes," added another, "we worked very hard designing the school curriculum for our youngsters."

"Maybe," responded a third elder, "we should relook at our school curriculum and decide how to improve student engagement in school." Taking that suggestion under consideration, the group of elders decided to reconvene the next day back at the local stream and choose one major attribute as the focus for the school and its curricula.

After some deliberation and prolonged disagreements, the elders decided they needed to hire an educational consulting firm to guide the direction of the new school. The firm had an eager beaver as the president, a curious cat as the vice president, and a playful otter as the director of professional development. The firm suggested that establishing provisions for student choice should be the essential element to the school's success and academic achievement. Along with that, the consultants made a case for revising the curriculum to feature differentiated instruction—where each and every teacher would design courses that complemented students' individual learning styles, abilities, and interests. The elders subsequently formed a communitywide committee to work with the consulting firm and the teachers at the school to revise their current "one-size-fits-all" methodology and to offer an array of elective courses in addition to running, climbing, swimming, and flying. The groundhog petitioned the committee to have digging added to the curriculum, and the owl suggested a night school since she slept most of the daylight hours. Both ideas were unanimously accepted by the school committee.

Differentiated instruction became a major shift in the day-to-day workings of the animal school. The otter introduced a "culture shift" for the new school and provided workshops on rebuilding the curriculum. School leaders learned how to build choice into classroom routines that supported student ownership and success. Teachers also learned how to enlist students as partners in implementing a structure that supported instructional choice, enabling all partners to meet expectations and standards that endorsed the school's new culture. At first, there were some challenges to the school's new direction, but after a while, the entire school community marshaled their energies into creating a learner-centered school. No longer were the teachers to be pigeonholed into a one-size-fits-all approach of teaching. As the new school year began, the school committee posted a sign inside the entrance of the school. It read, "A mind that is stretched by a new experience can never go back to its old dimensions.—Oliver Wendell Holmes"

A MOST DAUNTING TASK

The abilities to inquire, question, discover, and express innovative ideas are critical competencies for 21st-century schools—animals and human! Being on the brink of a new decade, science educators have the capacity to make these next 10 years the decade of differentiation in science instruction, a key concept in the National Research Council's (1996) *National Science Education Standards*, which espouse differentiated science inquiry methodology through the statements identified in the "Science Teaching" section of the standards. Those standards suggest teachers of science should do the following:

- Select science content and adopt and design curricula to meet interests, knowledge, understanding, abilities, and experience of students (p. 30).
- Challenge students to accept and share responsibility for their own learning (p. 36).
- Recognize and respond to student diversity and encourage students to participate fully in science learning (p. 36).
- Create a setting for student work that is flexible and supportive of science inquiry (p. 44).
- Enable students to have a significant voice in decisions about the content and context of their work, and require students to take responsibility for the learning of all its members of the community (p. 46).

THE ELEMENT OF TRUST

As classroom teachers adopt new pedagogies such as inquiry-based learning, differentiated teaching, and opportunities for choice (as advocated by the *National Science Education Standards* you just read), students will need to develop an element of trust that their teachers have their best interests in mind. As students are led to these new modes of learning, they too will need to alter their stance from a suspicious to a trusting acceptance that they are being prepared to cope in a world necessitating problem-solving skills. If there were a Periodic Table of Science Inquiry, the element of trust would have the symbol "Tr" and be placed between the elements Skepticism (Sk) and Understanding (Un).

Like inquiry, trust is both a noun and a verb. Trust means placing confidence or reliance in someone or something. Trust instills an expectation of integrity, a state (or hope) in which we rely on for some future event. According to Tomlinson (2008), "Trust begins when students believe that the teacher is on their side—when they realize that the teacher views them as persons of worth, believes in their capacity to succeed, and works in their best interest. Trust develops as students become aware that what goes on in the classroom supports their success individually and as a group" (p. 28).

A CALL FOR COMMITMENT

To avoid progressing at a snail's pace, science leaders, curriculum developers, and education reformers need to accelerate efforts to integrate differentiation and scientific inquiry into all aspects of the school's science program. What's now needed is a "call for commitment" that creates a momentum to transform the conventional status quo to the contemporary reforms. Taking a minimalist approach will never sharpen our students' competitive edge in the global marketplace. Science educators need to be aggressive in pursuing opportunities to develop competencies in science inquiry and differentiated science instruction as performance multipliers—moving from "me" to "we." It is a daunting task that will require undaunted courage.

The call to action from the national science standards requires acts of self-discovery and response from science educators. In reality, both entail a personal reflection that only you, as an individual, can do. So first, ask yourself the question: Am I ready to give up on the "one-size-fits-all" model and commit the time and effort to differentiate my science lessons to meet the needs of individual students? If the answer is "No," you just wasted money and time buying and reading this book. If the answer is "Yes," you'll need to find a quiet spot and spend some quality time to rethink your role as a teacher of today and tomorrow. Consider what it means to be a differentiated science teacher. Taking time to rediscover the kind of teacher you want to be is an essential aspect of your transformation. On a pad of paper or a journal, write down what you value as a teacher and think about how your values, beliefs, and biases are reflected in your classroom. Your notes will become invaluable as you progress through your professional metamorphosis.

As your own role as a teacher evolves, you will need to transform your science curriculum toward differentiated science inquiry, a professional venture that is certainly both ambitious and controversial. It is bound to be met with both curiosity and skepticism. To deal with both in a healthy, supportive manner, you can form professional learning communities—groups of teachers with similar goals—that can read articles and books on scientific inquiry and differentiation, share instructional successes, reflect with one another on emerging pedagogy, and journal individual progress toward reaching these goals. One means of modeling a commitment to differentiated inquiry can come in the form of sharing your ideas and successes. As you redesign your present investigations into a DSI format, consider sharing your revised activities and labs with other inquiry-based science teachers. By sending your DSI investigations to me at dllewell@rochester.rr.com or dllewellyn@sjfc.edu, they can be posted and disseminated on a DSI website where others can access and model your work.

In the next section, you will read about one high school science teacher who took the plunge into differentiation and found both the inspiration and the aspiration that separates the dreamers from the doers.

THE STORY OF LINZI PARK

Linzi Park describes herself as a typical fifth-year high school science teacher. She graduated from a prominent Midwestern university with an undergraduate degree in secondary science education, began teaching at Northbrook High School, and at 26 years old, embarked on a graduate program to deepen her knowledge of teaching and learning. Halfway through her master's program, she described her classes at Northbrook as well managed, but like many other teachers, was still trying to find her "niche" in teaching and questioned whether her current methods were where she would like them to be. At times, she felt her lessons were too prescriptive and too geared toward memorizing science facts and vocabulary terms for the sake of an end-of-the-year standardized test. She doubted if all her "drill and kill" lessons would prepare the students for life after high school graduation. Linzi felt she was sending students mixed messages—by purporting to have them think like a scientist while at the same time imparting a regiment of concepts to learn, only to be forgotten after the unit test was graded and handed back. Linzi asked herself if the students were essentially marionettes dancing to the teacher's instructional strings as to what they should know, how they should learn it, and how they should demonstrate what they were taught versus what was actually learned and retained.

Her graduate coursework offered a fresh, constructivist perspective in teaching and learning. Initially, she contemplated the idea of differentiation and a multiple-choice methodology with a degree of trepidation;

however, with some gentle prodding from a college professor, Linzi came to realize that the instructional path of lecturing first, discussing second, and assigning a confirmation lab third stymied her efforts to do what's best for learners.

Driving home from school one rainy Friday afternoon, Linzi started to ponder her legacy as a teacher. As the windshield wipers swayed in a hypnotic synchronism, she asked herself, "What would my high school graduates say about me years from now? Would I be the teacher that students always dreaded, or would I be the teacher students returned to high school to thank for how well I prepared them for the competitive world after Northbrook?" Little did she realize that these questions would eventually lead her to reexamine her purpose as a teacher and help her to find renewed meaning to her teaching.

Six months after that drizzly drive home, Linzi attended a local science educators' conference. At the conference, she heard a speaker present a session on differentiated science inquiry. Although she was immediately captivated with the idea, "what if" thoughts rushed through her head. . . .

- What if students baulk at the notion of choice?
- What if they choose a station based on what their friends choose and not their particular learning style or need?
- What if choice leads to imbalanced numbers of students at each station?
- Will this take more equipment and supplies than I have available?
- Are students prepared to accept that much choice and freedom in school?
- Oh my gaud, how can I manage three or four investigations going on simultaneously? This will certainly instill mass chaos in my classes. What will my department head think?

The answers to these and other questions would come gradually over time. For now, Linzi realized she needed to take an initial step toward varying her teaching style and work in stages on the mechanics of differentiation. It was the spring of 2008, and Linzi knew that once the 2009 school year began, she would test out her new outlook on teaching and learning.

For Linzi Park, the 2009 school year at Northbrook High School started like all the others. For the first month, her lessons followed the typical format of lecturing, discussing, and then assigning a prescribed lab. She realized that it was not surprising that she followed this classic sequence of teaching; after all, it was how she herself was taught in high school and the form of instruction her undergraduate science courses in college taught her to use. It too was the way most of her colleagues in the science department at Northbrook taught.

In November, however, students began noticing a slight change in the way they were learning science. Many of the science lessons started with the students observing a demonstrated inquiry that often had a surprising ending that left them nearly flabbergasted. The ending seemed to be a way to capture students' attention and lead them into asking engaging "what if" questions. Linzi then introduced the opportunity for choice and offered ways students could investigate their follow-up questions through structured and guided inquiries. The lecture and discussion portions of the class remained important aspects of the lesson but followed the inquiry as a means for students to analyze their results, make meaning of their new discoveries, and to connect their explanations to real-world situations. Her lectures were no longer a justification to preteach scientific terms and vocabulary before students had a chance to explore the lab concepts on their own. Lectures now reaffirmed what they learned and experienced.

At the start of the second semester, Linzi was assigned several special needs students to her second-period class. This, at the outset, concerned her since she already had several high-needs, struggling students in that class. Now, four more students were slated to be added. A benefit of the added students meant Linzi would have another teacher in the room to assist with the new students. Linzi Park was now paired with Tricia Brown, the school's resource teacher. Both were young and energetic and willing to collaboratively team teach science. Linzi became the science specialist, while Tricia assumed the role of the intervention specialist.

Tricia immediately adapted to Linzi's preliminary attempts in differentiation. Now the notion of varying instructional strategies for meeting diverse student needs seemed more imperative than ever before. Both teachers embraced implementing a multiple-choice methodology. Soon, Park and Brown put differentiated inquiry into full swing by designing a series of lessons that were introduced with a demonstrated inquiry, followed by a choice of both structured and guided inquiries. Giving students the freedom and flexibility of choice eventually led to greater cooperation among the class members and a tangible spirit of collaboration.

By April, the "dynamic duo" (as they were called by the students) were designing science lessons starting with an introduction and followed by four options: Structured Inquiry Choice 1, Structured Inquiry Choice 2, Guided Inquiry Choice 1, and Guided Inquiry Choice 2. Linzi often commented on how well the differentiating process succeeded with two teachers working together. In May, just after team teaching for three months, Linzi and Tricia planned their first four-station differentiated inquiry. The unit of study included a choice of inquiry approaches. In one classroom, Tricia led six students through a demonstrated inquiry in the front of the room, while three students worked on their own self-directed investigation in the back. Across the hall, Linzi watched over two groups: one group of six students doing a structured inquiry in one corner, with eight students who chose the guided inquiry approach working in another corner.

For her master's thesis, Linzi will use the year at Northbrook as an action research project to document her continued progress in implementing a differentiated science inquiry program. She will chronicle her journey with Tricia Brown and make anecdotal records of students' reaction to choice and accountability. To her master's advisor, she spoke about the transformation she is making: "Commitment to, and transformation through, DSI involves shedding 'old skins' and alters my understanding of the dimensions of scientific literacy. Moreover, it reconstructs my attitudes and beliefs about how students learn, what motivates them to learn, and the role they play in regulating their own learning. For me, transformation begins with paying attention to my intentions, and soon, with a bit of patience and practice, occasional, extraordinary science lessons become frequent, ordinary science lessons."

CLOSING THOUGHTS

As a closing thought, consider the ideas presented in this book not as answers and remedies but more like "seeds." Seeds that require planting, as well as loving and compassionate care during their germination phase. Hopefully, many of the seeds that you plant in your classroom will reap a harvest of fruitful experiences, for both you and your students. Cultivating your passion for inquiry will grow to be an inner realization that without inquiry, we teach as if nothing matters—except subject matter.

As a final point,

The purpose of inquiry is not to instill curiosity in students but to discover it; for curiosity and inquisitiveness already lie within the individual—awaiting opportunities to be revealed and made known.

D. Llewellyn
Rochester, New York

Resource A

Balls and Ramps Lesson Plan—Teacher Guide

Objective

To explore the concept of motion energy

Correlation to the **National Science Education Standards**, *Grades 5 Through 8:*

- Design and conduct a scientific investigation (p. 145).
- Develop descriptions, explanations, predictions, and models using explanations (p. 145).
- Think critically and logically to make the relationship between evidence and explanations (p. 145).
- The motion of an object can be described by its position, direction, and speed (p. 154).
- Unbalanced forces will cause changes in the speed of direction of an object's motion (p. 154).

Background Information for the Teacher

According to the National Research Council (NRC) (1996), "The study of motion and the forces causing motion provide concrete experiences on which a more comprehensive understanding of force can be based in Grades 9 through 12. By using simple objects, such as rolling balls and mechanical toys, students can move from qualitative to quantitative descriptions of moving objects and begin to describe the forces acting on the objects" (p. 154). In the Balls and Ramps stations, the amount of potential energy given to the balls is determined by the height of the release point. When the ball or marble is released, its potential energy is converted to kinetic energy (the motion of the ball). However, a significant amount of kinetic energy is "absorbed" as the ball hits the floor surface, especially when working on a carpeted area. Students will also investigate how the mass of the ball (wooden balls with various diameters) or marble affects the distance it will travel across the floor, realizing that the friction between the rolling ball and the floor's surface also affects the distance the ball rolls.

Possible Student Prior Conceptions

According to the NRC (1996), "Students think that friction, not inertia, is the principal reason objects remain at rest or require a force to move" (p. 154). In addition, to control for one variable, students may not understand that as the angle of the ramp increases, the release point of the ball should remain the same. Students may create a higher angle by increasing the number of blocks, thus also increasing the potential energy provided to the released ball.

Materials

- Assorted one-inch blocks (available in craft and hobby stores)
- 12-inch grooved rulers
- Assorted-size marbles (1/2", 3/4", 1")
- Assorted balls (ping-pong ball, super ball, rubber ball)
- Assorted wooden balls with different diameters (1/2", 3/4", 1", 2", 3", 4")
- Assorted steel balls with different diameters (1/2", 3/4", 1")
- Assorted golf balls (regular golf ball, Wiffle-type golf ball, hollow plastic golf ball)
- Measuring tapes
- Protractors
- Calculators (optional)
- Calipers for measuring the diameter of a marble or ball (optional)
- Triple-beam balances for measuring the mass of a marble or ball (optional)
- Science journals

Prior Setup and Arrangements

Arrange four separate stations in the room. Station A, the demonstrated inquiry, requires an additional person to conduct the demonstration. To avoid congestion, Station A could be set up in a separate room. Materials for each station should be readily available in a clear, plastic baggie or cardboard box. Describe to the class the procedure and the level of structure for each station. Emphasize that students have a choice in selecting their station. Allow the students to choose which station they prefer to complete based on their interest and need for structure.

Students Working in Groups

Students often dive into an investigation without spending the necessary time to completely understand or "noodle through" the question or problem being investigated. After all, for many youngsters, the best part of science is getting right into the materials. Encourage students to spend a considerable amount of time "getting to know" the question or problem facing them. Be sure students recognize the nature of the question before proceeding into the hands-on portion of the activity. Spending more time analyzing the question (and later reflecting on the question and its results) will enable students not only to *do* inquiry more effectively but also to better articulate and "come to know" *about* the process of scientific inquiry.

As students work in mixed groups (by ability, gender, language proficiency, or status), be observant and mindful as to which students have access to the materials and which role each is playing during the activity. When groups are mixed by gender, for example, two boys and two girls in a group, watch for the role that boys play versus the girls. Usually, boys tend to dominate the manipulative aspects of the investigation, leaving the observing and record-keeping role to the girls. This is especially true when the boys outnumber girls in a group, say, two boys and one girl in a group. Be sure each group member has equal access to the materials by distributing group roles and responsibilities equitably among the members.

With some groups, the teacher may decide to provide the hypothesis to test. With other groups, the teacher may want the students to formulate their own hypothesis. This will largely depend upon the experience level of the individuals within the group.

Students can also investigate how the length of the ramp, the surface of the flooring, the angle of the ramp, the diameter of the balls or marbles, the mass of the balls or marbles, the composition of the balls (glass, wood, or steel), or the release point on the ramp influences the distance the ball or marble will travel. It is especially important to know that many of the variables within this concept cannot be completely isolated. One variable may affect another. For example, as students vary the angle of the ramp (controlling for potential energy releasing the ball from a height of one block), they also vary the length of the ramp. Also, as the angle increases, much of the kinetic energy from the ball is "absorbed" by the floor when the ball reaches the end of the ramp.

For each station, the teachers may choose to add additional, unessential balls and marbles to the bag of materials. These will act as distracters, causing students to think critically about which materials are most appropriately needed to carry out the investigation and which are not. It may, however, trigger students to think that all the materials in the bag need to be used, thus causing students to test more than one variable at a time. Deciding which materials are relevant in an investigation is an essential reasoning skill in inquiry-based learning. Providing additional materials as distracters helps develop this fundamental skill.

As students carry out their procedure, they may ask, "What is the correct (or reasonable) number of trials to take?" The answer varies. Many science teachers recommend an odd number of trials, such as three or five, but certainly not one or two. In Stations A and B, the demonstrated and the structured inquiries, three trials are taken in order to determine an average. Teachers may choose to have advanced students make five trials and then eliminate the highest and lowest recordings and then report the range of the three trials plus the mean of the three middle distances.

If students have competence using Excel software, a computer-generated data table and a graph may be required.

Resource B

Balls and Ramps Lesson Plan—Student Guide

AS A STRUCTURED INQUIRY

Introduction

This investigation is designed as a structured inquiry where the problem and question and the procedure are provided, but collecting and organizing the results is left to you. This investigation provides a step-by-step procedure and the materials to complete each step. There are assorted balls and marbles in the bag of materials that will help you conduct this activity. At the end of the activity are several other questions you may choose to investigate.

Problem:

How does the height of an inclined plane affect the distance a marble will travel?

Materials:

- One 12-inch ruler with groove
- Five blocks (or books), each 2.5 cm or 1 inch high
- Several marbles
- One measuring tape
- Several sheets of graph paper

Procedure:

1. Place the 12-inch end of the ruler on the edge of a block.

2. Place the marble in the ruler's groove as far up the ruler as possible.

3. Release the marble.

4. Using that observation, make a prediction or hypothesis as to how the height of an inclined plane will affect the distance the marble travels. Record that statement on a separate sheet of paper.

   For example: My hypothesis is, "As the height of the ramp increases, the distance the marble travels will _____."

5. Repeat Steps 1 through 3 of the procedure for three separate trials. Using the measuring tape, measure the distance the marble travels for each trial.

6. In your journal, design a data table to record and organize the results.

7. Repeat the same procedure for two inches by placing a second block on top of the first. Place the ruler on the top of the second block so the height of the ruler is now at two inches. Release the marble and record your results in the data table.

8. Repeat the same procedure for three inches, four inches, and five inches and again, record your results in the data table.

9. Calculate the average for each height. Show your work.

10. Use the graph paper to graph your results. Be sure to provide a title to the graph and label the horizontal axis and vertical axes.

Conclusion: Using the data collected, decide if the prediction you made was correct or not and explain why. Place your explanation on the lines below.

_____

_____

_____

Follow-Up Investigation

In your science journal, design an investigation that will determine how the surface a ball or marble rolls on affects the distance it will travel. Include a diagram to illustrate your design. Place the question being investigated on a sentence strip and post it above the area where you complete your investigation. Carry out your investigation and record all important data. Be prepared to provide an explanation as to whether or not your prediction or hypothesis was correct.

Or you may choose to investigate any of the following questions:

- How will the distance the ball or marble travels be affected by shortening the ramp (ruler) from 12 inches to 6 inches? Or lengthening the ramp to 18 inches?
- How does the size of the marble (small, medium, and large) affect how far it will travel?
- How does the release point on the ruler affect the distance a ball or marble will travel?

AS A GUIDED INQUIRY

Introduction

This investigation is designed as a problem-solving activity or guided inquiry where the problem task is provided, but the procedure and collecting and organizing the results are left to you. This investigation provides five tasks and the materials to complete each task, although you probably may not complete all five tasks. There are assorted balls and marbles in the bag of materials that act as both distracters and enablers. In this case, rather than being told, you will have to determine which items you need and which items you don't need. The additional materials may also spur other questions and tasks to investigate.

To begin, follow the three steps listed below. From this initial exploration, choose one or more tasks from the list to investigate. For each task, write the question and a hypothesis on a sentence strip. Post the sentence strip on the wall above your work. Determine the variables and controls needed and design appropriate data tables to collect evidence for each investigation. Include a diagram to illustrate your investigation. Carry out your investigation and record all important data. Be prepared to provide an explanation as to whether or not your prediction or hypothesis was correct.

Procedure

1. Place one end of the ruler on the edge of a block.

2. Place the ball or marble in the ruler's groove as far up the ruler as possible.

3. Release the ball or marble.

Then, choose any one or more of the following tasks:

- Task 1: Design and carry out a procedure that will answer the question, "How does the height of an inclined plane affect the distance a ball or marble will travel?" Record all your data in your science journal.
- Task 2: Using the materials at the station, design and carry out a procedure that will have a small ball or marble, when released from the top of a ramp, stop precisely at a point five feet from the end of the ramp. Draw an illustration of your design. Record all your data in your science journal.
- Task 3: Repeat Task 2, this time using a golf ball instead of a small ball or marble. Answer the question, "How did you change the design of the procedure for Task 3?" Record all your data in your science journal.
- Task 4: Design and carry out a procedure that will answer the question, "How does the composition, diameter, or mass of a ball affect the distance it will travel?" Record all your data in your science journal.
- Task 5: Design and carry out an investigation to determine how the angle of a ramp or the surface of the floor affects the distance a marble will travel. Draw an illustration of the design and record all your data in your science journal.

AS A SELF-DIRECTED INQUIRY

Introduction

This investigation is a self-directed inquiry. Here, you will devise your own question, design and carry out the procedures to solve the question, and collect and organize evidence to support or refute the claim or hypothesis made from the question posed. There are assorted balls and marbles in the bag of materials that act as both distracters and enablers. Not all the supplies in the bag need to be used. You will have to determine which items you need to complete the task. The additional materials are expected to stimulate questions to investigate. To begin, follow these three steps:

Procedure

1. Place one end of the ruler on the edge of a block.

2. Place the ball or marble in the ruler's groove as far up the ruler as possible.

3. Release the ball or marble.

From this initial exploration, consider possible questions to investigate. Choose one question, and write a hypothesis for your investigation. Write both the question and the hypothesis on a sentence strip. Post the sentence strip on the wall above your work area. Determine the variables and constants needed, and design an appropriate data table to collect evidence for each investigation. Include a diagram to illustrate your investigation. Carry out your investigation and record all important data in your science journal. Be prepared to provide an explanation as to whether or not your prediction or hypothesis was correct as well as evidence to support or refute your hypothesis.

References

American Association for the Advancement of Science. (1993). *Benchmarks for science literacy*. New York: Oxford University Press.

Ashton, P. (1990). Teacher efficacy: A motivational paradigm for effective teacher education. *Journal of Educational Psychology, 82*(1), 33–40.

Bandura, A. (1997). *Self-efficacy: The exercise of control*. New York: Freeman.

Colburn, A. (2003). *The lingo of learning*. Arlington, VA: NSTA Press.

Deci, E., & Flaste, R. (1995). *Why we do what we do*. New York: Penguin Books.

Deci, E., & Ryan, R. (1982). *Curiosity and self-directed learning: The role of motivation in education*. ERIC Clearinghouse on Elementary and Early Childhood Education, Urbana, IL. (ERIC Document No. ED 206 377).

Deci, E., & Ryan, R. (1985). *Intrinsic motivation and self-determination in human behavior*. New York: Plenum.

Erwin, J. (2004). *The classroom of choice: Giving students what they need and getting what you want*. Arlington, VA: ASCD.

Gardner, H. (1999). *Intelligence reframed: Multiple intelligences for the 21st century*. New York: Basic Books.

Gregory, G., & Chapman, C. (2002). *Differentiated instructional strategies*. Thousand Oaks, CA: Corwin.

Gregory, G., & Hammerman, E. (2008). *Differentiated instructional strategies for science, grades K–8*. Thousand Oaks, CA: Corwin.

Guskey, T., & Anderman, E. (2008, November). Students at bat. *Educational Leadership, 66*(3), 8–14.

Hennessey, B. (2000). Rewards and creativity. In C. Sanone & J. Harackiewicz (Eds.), *Intrinsic and extrinsic motivation: The search for optimal motivation and performance* (pp. 55–77). San Diego, CA: Academic Press.

Jensen, E. (1998). *Teaching with the brain in mind*. Alexandria, VA: ASCD.

Karplus, R., & Their, H. (1967). *A new look at elementary school science*. Chicago: Rand McNally.

King-Shaver, B., & Hunter, A. (2003). *Differentiated instruction in the English classroom*. Portsmouth, NH: Heinemann.

Kneidel, S. (1993). *Creepy crawlies and the scientific method*. Golden, CO: Fulcrum Publishing.

Kohn, A. (1999). *Punished by rewards*. Bridgewater, NJ: Replica Books.

Liem, T. (1987). *Invitations to science inquiry*. Chino Hills, CA: Science Inquiry Enterprises.

Llewellyn, D. (2005). Measurement stations. *Science Scope, 29*(1), 18–21.

Llewellyn, D. (2007). *Inquire within: Implementing inquiry-based science standards in grades 3–8* (2nd ed.). Thousand Oaks, CA: Corwin.

Lumsden, L. (1994). *Student motivation to learn* (Report No. EDO-EA-94-7). Eugene, OR: Clearinghouse on Educational Management. (ERIC Document Reproduction Service No. ED99-C0–0011).

Marshall, J. (2008). *Overcoming student apathy: Motivating students for academic success*. Lanham, MD: Rowman & Littlefield.

National Research Council. (1996). *National science education standards*. Washington, DC: National Academy Press.

National Research Council. (2007). *Taking science to school: Learning and teaching science in grades K–8*. Washington, DC: National Academy Press.

Ogle, D. (1986). K-W-L: A teaching model that develops active reading of expository text. *The Reading Teacher, 39*(6), 564–570.

Robertson, W. (2002). *Force and motion: Stop faking it!* Arlington, VA: NSTA Press.

Ryan, R., & Deci, E. (2000). Intrinsic and extrinsic motivation: Classic definitions and new directions. *Contemporary Educational Psychology, 25,* 54–76.

Shields, M. (2006). *Biology inquiries*. San Francisco: Jossey-Bass.

Stipek, D. (2002). *Motivation to learn: Integrating theory and practice* (4th ed.). Boston: Allyn & Bacon.

Sullo, B. (2007). *Activating the desire to learn*. Alexandria, VA: ASCD.

The Access Center. (n.d.). *Differentiated instruction for science*. Retrieved December 11, 2008, from http://www.k8accesscenter.org/training_resources/sciencedifferentation.asp.

Thompson, R., & Carmack, E. (2007). Investigating minerals: Promoting integrated inquiry. *Science Activities, 44*(2), 56–60.

Tobias, S. (1994). Interest, prior knowledge, and learning. *Review of Educational Research, 64,* 37–54.

Tomlinson, C. (1999). *The differentiated classroom: Responding to the needs of all learners*. Alexandria, VA: ACSD.

Tomlinson, C. (2008, November). The goals of differentiation. *Educational Leadership, 66*(3), 26–30.

Tomlinson, C., & Kalhfleisch, M. (1998). Teach me, teach my brain: A call for differentiated classrooms. *Educational Leadership, 56*(3), 52–55.

Vygotsky, L. (1978). *Mind in society: The development of higher psychological processes*. Boston: Harvard University Press.

White-McNulty, L., Patrikakou, E., & Weissberg, R. (2005). *Fostering children's motivation to learn*. Philadelphia: Mid-Atlantic Regional Educational Laboratory. (ERIC Document Reproduction Service No. ED497147).

Wlodkowski, R. (1999). Motivating diversity: A framework for teaching. In M. Thell (Ed.), *Motivation from within: Approaches for encouraging faculty and students to excel* (p. 7). San Francisco: Jossey-Bass.

Index

CORWIN

A SAGE Company

The Corwin logo—a raven striding across an open book—represents the union of courage and learning. Corwin is committed to improving education for all learners by publishing books and other professional development resources for those serving the field of PreK–12 education. By providing practical, hands-on materials, Corwin continues to carry out the promise of its motto: **"Helping Educators Do Their Work Better."**